PRAISE FOR *AGENTS OF CHANGE*

"This immensely readable book tells the nearly lost stories of everyday women who dared to enter the man's world of the CIA and do extraordinary things. *Agents of Change* is a breath of fresh air into an obviously secretive and murky environment. I wish I had read Christina's book prior to my CIA career, as it would have assisted immeasurably with my understanding of that complicated world I was entering as a young woman. I'm thankful it's finally here."

> —**Valerie Plame**, *New York Times* **bestselling author of**
> ***Fair Game* and former CIA operations officer**

"A much-needed addition to spy literature that could only be written by someone who worked behind the veil. Bravo!"

> —**Pete Earley**, *New York Times* **bestselling author of**
> ***Confessions of a Spy: The Real Story of Aldrich Ames***
> **and** *Comrade J: The Untold Secrets of Russia's Master*
> *Spy in America After the End of the Cold War*

"*Agents of Change* is an important, groundbreaking piece of research, capturing the reality for generations of women who worked at the CIA. A must-read for historians, intelligence scholars, and any woman considering a career in national security."

> —**Alma Katsu**, **retired CIA officer and author of** *Red*
> *Widow* **and** *Red London*

"Hillsberg uses her insider knowledge to take us behind the curtain on the world of espionage, exposing far more than gender inequality—the compelling storytelling is a call to action and provides a map for moving forward. Meticulously researched and impeccably told, *Agents of Change* is a must-read."

> —**Eve Rodsky**, *New York Times* **bestselling author of**
> *Fair Play*

"An earth-shattering account of the badass women of the CIA that's equal parts infuriating and inspiring. Hillsberg holds the spy organization's feet to the fire, demanding accountability for the decades-long toxic culture of masculinity and sexual assault."

—Jo Piazza, bestselling author, podcast creator, and award-winning journalist

"An eye-opening exposé into the guts and grit it takes to be a woman in the CIA. Hillsberg interweaves the stories of trailblazing women with her own experience to give readers a front-row seat to the trials and triumphs of life undercover."

—Jessica Pearce Rotondi, author of *What We Inherit: A Secret War and a Family's Search for Answers*

"A revealing account of the discriminatory practices women faced in attempting to serve as intelligence officers in the CIA. The work highlights the individual careers of several woman agents who overcame these systemic practices and were able to carve out successful careers. Hillsberg has done a lasting service by bringing these facts out in the open so we can ensure that such practices will not raise their ugly head again."

—Frank Storey, former Deputy Assistant Director in Charge, FBI, and author of *The FBI's War Against the Mafia*

"Bold, brilliant, and beautifully written. Christina Hillsberg, a former CIA officer, charts women's captivating and challenging history in the CIA. Told with great verve, Hillsberg ensures women's voices are heard and their extraordinary contributions and experiences recorded, confirming her place as an important 'agent of change.'"

—**Claire Hubbard-Hall, author of *Secret Servants of the Crown: The Forgotten Women of British Intelligence***

"'Trailblazers and troublemakers' is how Hillsberg describes female pioneers at the CIA—and was there ever a more apt dichotomy? With compassion, insight, empathy, and courage, Hillsberg maps the challenges, heartbreak, accomplishments, and—most importantly—the human side of women navigating and building today's preeminent intelligence organization. *Agents of Change* is not just a compelling and eye-opening read, but serious scholarship and a cautionary road map that will prove to be a vital piece of this much-neglected area of history."

—**I. S. Berry, award-winning author of *The Peacock and the Sparrow* and former CIA intelligence officer**

Books by
CHRISTINA HILLSBERG

License to Parent:
How My Career as a Spy Helped Me Raise
Resourceful, Self-Sufficient Kids

Agents of Change:
The Women Who Transformed the CIA

AGENTS OF CHANGE

THE WOMEN WHO TRANSFORMED THE CIA

CHRISTINA HILLSBERG

CITADEL PRESS
KENSINGTON PUBLISHING CORP.
KENSINGTONBOOKS.COM

First Citadel hardcover printing: July 2025

Printed in the United States of America

ISBN: 978-0-8065-4349-9

ISBN: 978-0-8065-4351-2 (e-book)

Library of Congress Control Number: 2025933136

The authorized representative in the EU for product safety and compliance is eucomply OU, Parnu mnt 139b-14, Apt 123, Tallinn, Berlin 11317; hello@eucompliancepartner.com

For our girls

Don't let somebody tell you, for whatever reason, you can't do it because you're a woman.

—PATTY, CIA operations officer (1973–2004)

The reason I'm talking to you is because I don't want future generations of young women to have the experience I've had here. I want this place to be better for other women.

—ELYSE, CIA collection management officer (2015–2023)

CONTENTS

Foreword by Valerie Plame xiii

Author's Note xvii

Introduction: Sacrifice and Gumption 1

CHAPTER 1 The Secretarial Sixties 11

CHAPTER 2 The Second-Wave Seventies 29

CHAPTER 3 The Empowering Eighties. 55

CHAPTER 4 The Promising Yet Problematic Nineties 77

CHAPTER 5 The Terrorism-Driven 2000s 115

CHAPTER 6 The Groundbreaking 2010s. 141

CHAPTER 7 2020 and Beyond 173

Epilogue 189

Glossary 197

Acknowledgments 201

Notes 205

Discussion Questions 219

FOREWORD

By Valerie Plame

As a former covert CIA operations officer, I've been waiting for someone to write *Agents of Change*, and I'm so glad Christina Hillsberg tackled it with verve, intelligence, and competency. When I joined the CIA, there was no internet and there were few books available on the Agency, much less about the women who served. The stories I heard of women who worked in the field recruiting agents were shadowy: bits and pieces of bravery, audacious actions, and how our male counterparts at times reacted very badly to these trailblazers. I was still under the innocent and naive assumption that men and women were going to be treated equally and fairly in a professional environment. However, it quickly became apparent that was not the case. For example, my male counterparts routinely got the "hot prospect" leads that in most cases a woman could have recruited and handled just as well (if not better). The alpha male managers saw reflections of their younger selves in the men and appeared genuinely confounded by the appearance of women in the case officer cadre. I had no idea of the history of women in the CIA that I walked into. In the early years of my career, I was so consumed with my own ambitions that it took time for me to connect the dots and realize that my own trajectory was built upon those intrepid women who had come before. It is obvious that the women serving in the Agency today owe a huge debt of gratitude to those who showed the way and shouldered some of the worst transgressions.

Agents of Change upends all that—this immensely readable book tells the nearly lost stories of everyday women who dared to enter the man's world of the CIA and do extraordinary things. At times, they had to make impossible choices between caring for their children and families and the demands of a strange but deeply satisfying job. Christina has scored exclusive interviews with former and current CIA officers who have never spoken publicly about their careers, the pride they took in their work, and the sacrifices they made to do so.

Set against the backdrop of the larger women's movement that gathered momentum in the 1960s up until today, Christina tells their stories as an insider herself and as an excellent researcher. Larger societal trends of women in the workforce took longer to permeate into the CIA and were slowed significantly by a male-dominated bureaucracy that did not see the value or frankly the need for women to serve in field positions around the world. I recall looking for women who had reached senior levels of the Agency (SIS, or Senior Intelligence Service— equivalent to flag rank in the military) for potential mentors. It was a depressingly small group, and even fewer in operations.

The CIA came late to the notion that diversity in the work- force is a good thing. It didn't seem to occur to management that the spies we wanted to recruit might respond better to someone other than a white American male graduate from a top US university. Women were not hired as case officers specif- ically until the end of the seventies. The women who did serve in those positions most likely worked as secretaries or in other administrative roles until they badgered, pleaded, or found a male mentor to encourage and shepherd them into proper ops roles. Today, the Agency does value diversity in its workforce, but let's just say it's still a work in progress. It's not good enough to recruit a diverse workforce; after pouring significant taxpayer monies into their training, the CIA must retain them. Otherwise, that expensive and elusive talent walks out the door to a more welcoming and inclusive work environment.

Christina exposes several tales of egregious sexual harassment and sexual assault that appear to have been mishandled by the Agency, which is both heartbreaking and baffling to read. To continue to attract top-shelf talent, the organization clearly needs to do a better job at addressing these genuine concerns and applying justice. The women who serve, just like their male counterparts, do so out of a deep sense of patriotism (it's not the money!). They deserve respect and clear rules that if broken bring severe consequences. It's called institutional accountability, and it is essential for our national security that these issues are taken seriously with transparency and resources.

Agents of Change is a breath of fresh air into an obviously secretive and murky environment. The women Christina chose to write about leap off the page and are instantly relatable with their career desires, setbacks, daunting choices, and raw talents in an esoteric field. I knew some of these women and am in awe of their accomplishments despite serious headwinds. The agents of change *are* these remarkable women working to make necessary changes from within. I wish I had read Christina's book prior to my CIA career, as it would have assisted immeasurably with my understanding of that complicated world I was entering as a young woman. I'm thankful it's finally here, and it will be appreciated by many, both inside the Agency and out. It's my honor to introduce *Agents of Change*, which fills a long-neglected gap in the Agency's history.

AUTHOR'S NOTE

When I embarked on this book, my goal was to write the kind of pop history of the women of the CIA that I would want to read. A book that appealed to readers beyond spy aficionados and history buffs. Simply put, I wanted to tell the stories of ordinary women at the CIA doing extraordinary things. I knew I'd be tackling gender discrimination issues, but I didn't anticipate discussing sexual harassment and sexual assault. My research and countless interviews with current and former CIA officers, however, uncovered a pervasive pattern that I felt compelled to include.

While my experience working as a woman at the Agency has its benefits—I have exclusive access to individuals and a knowledge of the inner workings of the organization—I'm also keenly aware that I bring my own biases to my reporting, both conscious and unconscious. However, it's been my sincere goal to strike a balance and be as thorough and objective as possible in my reporting, even at times when it felt challenging. I've sought to give the CIA credit where credit is due because, despite the problems that may remain, there has been tremendous progress when it comes to the role of women at the organization. At the same time, I haven't shied away from the more difficult times in the CIA's history when it comes to women or some of the more troubling issues still occurring at the Agency today.

This book is the culmination of three years of extensive research and interviews with dozens of current and former CIA intelligence officers—women and men—and draws from my own experience at the Central Intelligence Agency. The sections that feature specific women are based on firsthand accounts with the exception being when the woman has already passed away, in which case I have interviewed close friends, family, and colleagues to create as close to an accurate portrayal as possible.

While these interviews have included officers from across directorates at the CIA, I have chosen to devote the bulk of the book to women who have served in the Directorate of Operations (DO). As someone who spent the first part of my career as an analyst in the Directorate of Intelligence (DI), now called the Directorate of Analysis (DA), and the latter half in the DO, I can tell you that I never felt the remnants of the old boys' club more strongly than I did when I was in the DO. It's also the part of the organization that I believe has seen—and needed—the most change with regard to women's roles and contributions through the decades.

This book is also informed by firsthand, in-person interviews at CIA headquarters with women from across directorates, the director of the CIA Museum, and the Agency's Talent and Acquisition team. I've worked closely with the CIA's Pre-publication Classification Review Board to ensure I do not inadvertently disclose classified information, a requirement for former CIA officers.

I've chosen to refer to many of the women in this book by their first names, rather than last names, in an effort to make them more relatable, bring them to life on the page, and protect national security. For instances when I've used a pseudonym,

I've noted it with an asterisk next to the name upon first mention. If given permission by the individual and the CIA, I've included true names. In some instances, I've only been granted permission to use a true *first* name. When necessary, I've obfuscated identifying details to protect CIA officers' cover status and national security. Lastly, I've used the terms "case officer" and "operations officer" interchangeably.

INTRODUCTION

SACRIFICE
AND GUMPTION

I needed to be absolutely certain I wasn't under surveillance when I arrived at the meeting, so I didn't take a direct route to my final destination in Western Europe. I first traveled by plane to another country, where I conducted a circuitous surveillance detection route on foot through the city and made my way to the train station. From there, I took a train to my final destination. I was traveling as a tourist, so I built in a few days in the city to explore museums to sell my cover. If I was under the watchful eye of the country's local security services, I needed to make them believe I was actually a tourist—not an undercover CIA operative. From there, I headed north of the city to the small village where we agreed to meet. I sat in the back of a dimly lit pub with a clear view of the door, anxiously awaiting my asset's arrival and the secrets he'd bring with him.

It was the last clandestine operation I would conduct during my career at the CIA. I was nearly a decade in, and I knew at the end of this tour, I would resign. But before I did, I'd have this one last meeting with an asset I had grown to respect and even develop a genuine friendship with over the years. He also happened to be best positioned to report on a contentious foreign presidential election of interest to policymakers back home, making him an important case for the CIA station where I was posted. What's more, he was smart and funny to boot, both qualities that can't be underestimated when you're spending hours debriefing an asset for intelligence.

When I looked up from my menu to see him walking through the front door of the pub, I was struck with relief. There's always a chance that an asset won't show up for a third-country meeting, and although he hadn't covertly signaled to me that he wouldn't be there, I knew all too well that when it comes to espionage, things can always change. We greeted each other like any old friends meeting in a pub would and exchanged pleasantries over pints of beer while I gave him specific instructions on when and where to meet me next.

I booked a room at a nearby hotel with plenty of built-in look-backs along the way to ensure he didn't inadvertently bring surveillance with him to the meeting. There was no such thing as being too careful. Any association with the CIA could put him and his family at serious risk—not to mention the possibility of my getting arrested. My tourist persona didn't afford me protection. I carefully slid a key to the hotel room across the table before leaving the pub and beginning my next surveillance detection route on foot toward the hotel—the place where, in just a few hours, my asset would divulge everything he knew about his country's elections.

When I began my career at the CIA as a fresh-faced twenty-one-year-old college graduate in 2006, I hit the ground running. Another conflict was heating up in East Africa, and I was writing about it in our premier intelligence product, the

President's Daily Brief, or PDB. Soon, I traveled, undercover and almost always alone, to CIA stations across the globe. Sometimes the travel was for meetings to support my intelligence analysis, and other times, I spent countless hours in secure, covert locations providing highly classified linguistic support to keep the president safe. Years later, when I transitioned from the Directorate of Intelligence (DI) to the Directorate of Operations (DO), I ran my own cases, meeting with clandestine assets and collecting foreign intelligence of national security interest in the field.

I knew things hadn't always been this way—the CIA was long known as an old boys' club, and I was keenly aware that there was a time, decades in fact, that these opportunities hadn't come as easily for women. Director of Central Intelligence (DCI) Allen Dulles recognized decades ago the disparities in pay and position between male and female employees and in 1953 commissioned what would become known as the Petticoat Panel. The report uncovered significant inequities between men and women. The average grade for women was a GS-5, whereas for a man, it was GS-9. (GS means "General Schedule," the pay system for the majority of civilian Federal employees, although it is commonly referred to as "Grade Step.") Not a single woman held a senior executive position or an office higher than branch chief. And only 7 percent of branch chiefs were women. Despite such revelations, the Agency stopped short of implementing any new policies to course correct, and it would take decades (and more decades after that) to see any real change. Twenty years later, for example, a woman was feigning being sterile just to be considered for an operations officer position that traditionally went to a man.

"I really don't believe in women being ops officers. You might get pregnant . . . and you'll have to take all that time off," a woman named Meredith's supervisor, the CIA deputy chief of

Europe, told her at Langley when she pressed him on why he didn't want to put her forward for an operations officer position.

"I've been fixed," she lied. Her manager proceeded to put her in for the position, and soon after, she promptly became pregnant on her first operational tour. She gave birth via cesarean section and was back out on the street running operations after just seven days.[1] "I wasn't the only one that was doing that—all of us," she said of her short postpartum recovery. "You really felt like you couldn't take off and do that."

Fifty years after the Petticoat Panel, I've found a new appreciation for these early female spies while reflecting on my career in espionage amid raising three daughters. Indeed, throughout my career at the Agency, I was surrounded by exceedingly clever and capable women. And it was their sacrifice and gumption that made it possible for me to forge the career that I did. I became curious about their stories: Who were they and why did they join the CIA? And what was it like being a woman at the Agency in the decades leading up to mine?

Sure, we may think we know the female spy. After all, we've seen her portrayed numerous times on-screen—often in the background or as a sidekick clad in a bikini with a knife on her hip. But the reality is that she's been playing a much larger role than we've given her credit for—from women like Eloise Page, who began as General William Donovan's secretary in the Office of Strategic Services (OSS) and rose to become the highest-ranking female employee in 1975, to Elizabeth Swanek, who joined in 1951, bringing with her a military background in signals communications, medical training, and Russian-language expertise. Swanek was sent to Germany, where she targeted and trained assets to infiltrate the Soviet Union; she went on to receive the CIA's Career Intelligence Medal. More recently, Gina Haspel led the CIA as its first female director beginning in 2018, and in 2021, for the first time, the Agency and all of its directorates were led by women. Even the chief of staff was a woman. For those of us who have worked in the shadows, there's no doubt that women have been, and continue to be, an integral part to what CIA officers affectionately call "the mission."

But similar to how the Bond Girl has evolved over time since Honey Ryder emerged from the water in that iconic white bikini in 1962's *Dr. No*, so too has the female intelligence officer. (I'll return to such comparisons at points throughout the book, to compare reality to the sometimes-contrasting impressions that the world received from popular culture at the same time in history.)

When the Bond Girl was born as a mere sexual associate of her more capable British male spymaster, women were deep in a war of gender politics across the pond at Langley. In fact, the assumption at CIA headquarters at the time was that any woman you came across at headquarters was a secretary or clerk. After all, when the CIA began, the bulk of its recruits were white men from the Ivy League. Even the most highly decorated female spy in history, Virginia Hall, whose intelligence contributions during World War II were instrumental, was confined to a desk at headquarters for fifteen years after the war, where she reportedly faced discrimination as a woman—passed over for promotions and career opportunities and answering to managers with far less experience in intelligence operations.[2]

The second wave of feminism continued into the seventies, birthing key milestones like the publication of Gloria Steinem's *Ms.* magazine and the Supreme Court's decision in *Roe v. Wade*. Around that time Gloria Hendry made history on-screen as the first Black woman romantically involved with Bond, but it was far from the heyday for Black women at the CIA in the seventies—and you might argue that day has yet to arrive. In fact, female—mostly white—intelligence officers were still trying to convince men to give them a shot at running their own operational cases in a battle against the old boys' network. Later, we'll discuss one woman who succeeded at this: Martha "Marti" Peterson became the first female case officer stationed in Moscow, in 1975, but not before boldly turning down two tours as an intelligence assistant.[3]

In the same way women at the CIA were bullishly proving their worth in espionage operations, no matter the cost, women continued to make gains elsewhere—on the Supreme Court, in space, and on television and in film. In 1983, actress Maud Adams appeared in all her skinny-dipping glory in the first Bond film named after its female protagonist, a step forward for women, if you could ignore that the actual title of the film was *Octopussy*. By this time, however, the number of female operations officers had increased at the Agency, and women were now focusing their efforts on securing sought-after recruitment cases. Interviews and archival materials suggest that the widely held belief among their male counterparts at that time was that women simply were not equipped to recruit assets—that is, formally ask a person to commit to a clandestine relationship with the CIA. And so, in a best-case scenario, they were given operational handling cases—maintaining relationships and debriefing assets who were already recruited for foreign intelligence—or safehouse management responsibilities.[4] But that started to change in the mid-eighties around the time when intrepid women set up the Directorate of Operations Women's Advisory Council (DOWAC).[5] And soon after, another group of women created a women's mentoring program that reached across Agency directorates.[6]

This momentum continued into the nineties—a decade full of significant strides for gender equality and yet fraught with problematic notions on the treatment of women. In the Bond world, it seemed they were moving closer to getting their depiction of the female spy right, and that was due in large

part to producer Barbara Broccoli, who is credited for bringing more balance and inclusivity to the films. At the same time,
it seemed women were on the verge of notable progress at the
CIA. The discrimination that women had been experiencing for
decades was brought to light with the publication of the CIA's
Glass Ceiling study in 1991. Seeing the statistics in black and
white made it difficult to deny that the Agency was dealing with
systemic bias and discrimination toward women and minorities. The study found that women were concentrated in lower
grades than men; for example, women made up 40 percent of
the workforce, yet they held only 10 percent of the Senior Intelligence Service (SIS) positions, the senior-most level at the CIA.
While it is unclear whether the study resulted in any immediate
strides toward go-forward salary parity, it did help pave the way
for a landmark gender discrimination win against the Agency
in 1994 and, a year later, a separate class action suit, in which
the CIA agreed to pay more than $1 million in back pay and
salary increases to settle charges of gender discrimination.

Women continued to make progress in their efforts to
achieve equality in the workplace in and outside of the Agency
into the twenty-first century, resulting in women in leadership
positions at the CIA and a notable uptick in female CEOs of
Fortune 500 companies by the end of the 2000s. The event that
would shape the decade, as well as change intelligence collection and national security as we knew it, was the attack on the
World Trade Center on September 11, 2001. And, as we'll discuss, female intelligence officers played key roles in tracking
terrorists and keeping America safe.

Amid a growing #MeToo movement in the 2010s, women
were advancing in arenas ranging from the military to politics to space exploration. In the same way they were making
gains politically, socially, and culturally in America, women
were continuing to make notable strides at the CIA, with the

first female director, Gina Haspel, in 2018, and the first female deputy director for operations, Elizabeth Kimber, elevated that same year. With the promotion of Cynthia "Didi" Rapp as deputy director for analysis, women found themselves at the helm of the three top CIA directorates for the first time ever.[7] (Dawn Meyerriecks had been serving as deputy director for science and technology since 2015.[8])

At least some aspects of such progress can be traced to a post-9/11 world in which the Agency was recruiting employees at a record pace. As of 2023, women made up 45 percent of the CIA workforce.[9] Still, the Agency continued to flounder in terms of recruiting, retaining, and promoting women of color. Langley reinvigorated its efforts to bring diversity to its ranks and even launched a new recruitment website in early 2021 devoted to hiring more diverse candidates, a top priority of Director Haspel,[10] but even today, minority women still make up only 13 percent of the Agency population.[11]

While their numbers may have not always been large, there's no doubt that the women of the CIA are a mighty force. When I set out to interview my former colleagues for this book, I had no idea how enthralled I would become with their stories. Theirs are the stories of women who sacrificed their personal lives, risked their safety, and devoted themselves to the CIA's mission. Marti, the first female intelligence officer to operate in Moscow, who was arrested and expelled from the country. Kathleen*, a first-generation Korean American immigrant, whose asset brought her the severed head of a terrorist in the trunk of his car. Denise, a nineteen-year-old secretary with a high school diploma, who proved her ability to run a CIA station after a coup d'état in West Africa prompted an evacuation of nearly all US personnel. Their accomplishments are nothing short of extraordinary, and it's my hope to shine a light on their impressive work in intelligence, while acknowledging the sometimes-challenging road it took to get here. Were these the same women with whom I walked the halls at Langley every day? The women whose paths I crossed in field stations in Africa and elsewhere around the world? It seemed I was so focused on getting ahead in my own career that I never stopped to look at the shoulders of those who came before me on which I stood.

Through exclusive interviews with current and former female intelligence officers, I'll share the untold story of how women proved their worth at the world's most powerful spy agency—from pioneering women in the sixties like Lucy, who graduated from Wellesley with the world seemingly at her feet, to today's female spies, like Mary*, a first-generation Lebanese American, whose family narrowly escaped civil war before immigrating to the United States. I'll begin each chapter with a discussion of women's issues during that decade before bringing to life the stories of female CIA operations officers, starting with the 1960s and working my way to the present. I'll examine what it meant to be a woman during that time and highlight why their experiences are emblematic of female spies in each given era.

Many of these women have never spoken publicly about their careers at the CIA, and they would never dream of speaking to a journalist about their clandestine operations. But I was one of them. As a former CIA officer, I know their world. I speak their language. And they've entrusted me with their stories—stories that, if left untold, will eventually be lost forever.

This book is not meant to be a comprehensive history of the CIA nor of women's biggest or most important contributions to intelligence. Nor is it meant to catalog the most accomplished female case officers, although they are all quite accomplished. Rather, I chose to focus my research on everyday women of the CIA who were doing extraordinary things. And making choices—at times impossible ones—related to their careers and families. They were breaking down barriers and shattering glass ceilings so that women like me could come along years later and reap the benefits. Some were considered the troublemakers of their time, even still to this day, and others, trailblazers. I like to think they're both. These are their stories.

CHAPTER 1

THE SECRETARIAL
SIXTIES

I t was the sixties. The women's liberation movement was taking hold in the United States, thanks in large part to the publication of Betty Friedan's *The Feminine Mystique*, which sold three million copies in only three years. Birth control was now legal. And the Bond Girl was born. Bond novels were already a phenomenon in Britain, and their portrayal of women and sex introduced a new kind of woman on-screen. With the benefit of more than fifty years of hindsight, it's easy to take aim at the one-dimensional female spy archetype, but at the time, it was considered progressive for a woman to show that type of sexual independence—if you can call it that. In today's world, it's difficult not to cringe when recalling the names of Bond Girls like Honey Ryder and Pussy Galore—or even worse, the scene in 1964's *Goldfinger* in which Bond forces himself on Pussy Galore in a hay-filled barn.

While the Bond Girl was born on-screen, women at the CIA weren't interested in being sexy sidekicks to their male counterparts. They wanted to run their own clandestine operations.

Women began participating in operational training at the CIA's covert training facility, the Farm, as early as 1961 in a course that was then called Junior Officer Training (JOT) program (and later, the Career Trainee program); however, only 4 percent of the officers were women. It would be several decades before that would change to any remarkable degree.[1] Several revolutionary legal reforms lay the groundwork for women to play larger roles in the workplace, including at the CIA. For example, the Equal Pay Act was passed in 1963, and a year later, Title VII of the Civil Rights Act followed. In 1965, a federal labor law restricting women's work hours was repealed, and in 1967, President Johnson's Executive Order 11375 broadened the affirmative action policy of 1965 to include discrimination based on gender. And in 1969, President Nixon signed Executive Order 11478, extending equal employment opportunity to federal government employees.[2]

The CIA was hiring women at the time, but throughout the sixties, the majority were placed in secretarial roles and other desk jobs, despite often being immensely qualified to do more, possessing skills like foreign languages and advanced degrees. One woman who interviewed with the CIA could fly an airplane and speak Mandarin, but her Agency recruiter was interested only in knowing whether she could type.[3]

Another woman, Debra*, found herself at the CIA as a last resort. She wanted to go to medical school, she explained, but when she made the rebellious decision to get married at nineteen years old to a spouse who didn't regularly work, she began applying to jobs with pharmaceutical companies who were looking for sales reps to market their products to physicians. With the legalization of birth control, there were a lot of jobs marketing the pill in the late sixties, she noted. The only problem? You had to be big enough to carry heavy sample cases.

And for Debra, who stood at only five two and weighed just over one hundred pounds, that wasn't an option.

"A lot of doors were closed because I was 'too little,'" she told me.

When Debra saw a stunning woman stand onstage at a career fair at her university, talking about the death of the president of Costa Rica and explaining that it was her job to advise the US president on whether we should recognize the new Costa Rican government, she was intrigued.

Debra began at the CIA months later and found it wasn't as glamorous as it sounded—at least not at first. The Vietnam War was getting hotter, and the Agency's role was escalating. But instead of the exciting picture she painted in her head, Debra was asked to alphabetize Vietnamese names.

"That was a big comedown," she told me.

Once her SCI/TK (short for sensitive compartment information/talent keyhole; it's broadly known in the intelligence community by its abbreviated form) clearance came through, she became involved in the Central Reference Service (CRS) as what was essentially a glorified librarian, but she didn't mind; she had worked in libraries before and loved books.[4]

A woman named Ann Donohue, now in her nineties, also found herself in a mundane typing role in personnel when she entered on duty, but she finally broke out of it in the early sixties when she volunteered for a temporary duty assignment (TDY) as a reports officer in Cairo. She became enthralled with the work and the idea of living overseas. When she returned to headquarters and once again found herself underutilized, she filled her time with training courses until the chief of Far East Division sponsored her to undergo operational training at the Farm and receive her field tradecraft certification, also referred to as an "ops certification."[5] She was one of three women in her

Farm class.[6] The prevailing view at the time was that women couldn't be operations officers because they had families—or would want to have families at some point—and the Agency (read: *male* CIA officers) didn't want to invest time and money into a woman who could get pregnant and leave the organization at a moment's notice. An actual personnel file from 1968 reads: "She's very bright and attractive, but she's young and very likely to get married and have children. Or get pregnant."[7] They viewed hiring women of childbearing age as a waste.[8,9] But it wasn't a waste; women like Lucy and Janine found themselves in operations and were ready to put their training to good use.

NAME: LUCY KIRK
YEAR OF BIRTH: 1940
PLACE OF BIRTH: COLUMBUS, OHIO
ENTRANCE ON DUTY (EOD): 1967
FIELD TRADECRAFT CERTIFICATION: YES
HOME BASE: CHINA OPS
FOREIGN LANGUAGES: FRENCH, SPANISH

Lucy was never told "You can't do that" while growing up, but even so, she came to realize over the years that there were some things women just didn't do. But that didn't stop her from trying—and accomplishing—many of those things.

Born to a traditional family in 1940 in Columbus, Ohio, Lucy had a mother who stayed at home while her father, a very serious man whom Lucy idolized, forged a career as a surgeon. Apart from her three younger brothers at home, Lucy was surrounded by young women; she attended Columbus School for Girls and later, Wellesley College, where she lived in the same dorm as Madeleine Albright, although she didn't know it at the time. It was there that Lucy gained an education as well as instructions and expectations on how to be a fine wife and a fine mother.[10] She graduated in 1962, just three years after Albright and seven years before Hillary Rodham Clinton, who in 1969 would give a groundbreaking graduation speech that would energize her female classmates on the cusp of entering a world that was ripe for change by the women's movement.[11,12,13]

After graduation, Lucy wanted to live in France—or anywhere overseas, really, she told me. She decided to go to Argentina, which she recalled her grandfather telling her was quite gutsy. While there, she lived with a local family in Buenos Aires and fell in love with the country and the idea of living abroad. When summer ended, Lucy returned to Boston, where she lived with five other Wellesley graduates. They were all dating men from Harvard Law and intent on finding a husband—no surprise, given that they came from a school where senior girls pushed hoops down a hill every May Day to see who would be the first to get married. Lucy was no exception in this regard. But despite her best efforts, she didn't fall in love.

And so, Lucy began to work at the Fletcher School at Tufts University. Her thirst for knowledge was palpable, prompting the dean to suggest she further her studies by applying to graduate school. She took his advice and was accepted to a master's program at American University in Washington, DC, where she'd study Latin American Studies, but not just yet. First, Lucy flew off for her next adventure—a summer with friends exploring Europe, East Germany, and Egypt. By fall, she arrived in Washington, where she'd spend the majority of the next two years studying and visiting the Library of Congress, soaking up everything she could. She was happy. She felt like a child again. But after finishing her master's degree, her father was growing tired of her continued interest in education and concerned that she was still unmarried.[14]

"I think you've had enough education," he told Lucy, along with a deadline. She was to be married by twenty-eight years old. Lucy found, however, that her yearning for an international career increasingly eclipsed her desire for a husband. She began going to any job interview that had the word "international" in it, and when a few male friends encouraged her to pursue a career with the CIA, she thought, *Why not?* When the CIA recruiter interviewing her told Lucy about the travel opportunities, she didn't need any convincing. She went home, improved her résumé, and took it back the next day. Except no one was there, so she mailed it in instead. After several months, she finally heard back, and in April 1967, she began her career at the CIA.[15]

Lucy first went to the short operational (ops) course as one of nine women in a class of ninety, which gave her exposure to operations but stopped short of giving her a full operational certification to become a case officer. Afterward, she went back to headquarters for interims in different parts of the Agency. While working on a Central America desk, she began to hear talk about what women "couldn't do." *You can't do this. You can't do that.* One of those things she learned women "couldn't do" was become an operations officer—the very position Lucy became intent on securing. In order to do so, she'd need to complete the long ops course to receive her field tradecraft certification, which included everything from learning surveillance detection, role-playing asset meetings, offensive and defensive driving, and weapons training—essentially all aspects of intelligence tradecraft. This course and resulting certification was a requirement for running operations, i.e., meeting and recruiting assets to collect foreign intelligence. However, as she and six other women were planning to return to the Farm to complete the long ops course, they began hearing rumors that women "couldn't run ops." And soon after, the women were told they weren't allowed to go. One of them, however, had already secured an overseas assignment. Her manager went to bat for all six of them, and the women were permitted to return to the Farm for the necessary training to receive their operational certification and become full-fledged operations officers. [16]

Lucy became fast friends with a woman named Pam in her Farm class. The two of them stayed up late studying and doing homework together, while the men socialized and played pool. Lucy and Pam soon realized many of the men just didn't do the homework. That wasn't an option for women at the Farm. With so few of them there, they knew they had to work hard if they wanted to be considered for the same opportunities. Each of the students was assigned a mentor, and one of Lucy's classmates warned her that hers was very flirty: a womanizer. With that in mind, Lucy went into her first agent meeting with him in one of the dorms prepared and quite serious. (As they still do today, the instructors posed as foreign assets in a fictitious country scenario, and most exercises consisted of role-playing.) When Lucy walked into the room, she immediately noticed that her male classmates had covered the walls with *Playboy* centerfolds, hoping to trip her up in her meeting. It didn't work. She took it in stride and, she recalled, at the time even found it rather funny. Later that evening, the men were reprimanded, but it didn't impact their careers. [17]

Lucy completed the long ops course at the Farm and upon returning to headquarters found herself homebased in China ops at the height of the Chinese Cultural Revolution. She was pleased with this placement, as she had never bought into the domino effect theory that Communists were taking over the world and knew that China and the Soviet Union were the "two big apples." It was a dark time in China—the Agency had no assets there. Lucy heard that it had resorted to talking to vegetable vendors to collect intelligence, which she was sure must be a cryptonym for assets. But she soon learned that the Agency was so desperate for intelligence that they were talking to people on street corners and essentially anyone they could find, including actual vegetable vendors. [18]

At the same time Lucy was getting her footing in China ops, she was dating a classmate from the Farm, and the two of them married in 1969. Her husband was in Africa Division, which changed everything for Lucy. While they continued to offer *him* jobs overseas, they didn't offer any to Lucy. There was no such thing as tandem couples at the time, and the expectation was that she would simply tag along with her husband on his assignment. [19]

"You'll get a job when you come back to Washington," a senior manager told Lucy when they were out to lunch one day. But that didn't sit well with her. She couldn't imagine lounging around doing nothing on an overseas tour when she had already passed the training to run her own clandestine operations. She even asked if she could use her skills informally as a housewife, but she was told no. She didn't admit it to herself at the time, but inside her, something was stirring. Rebelling, even. She wanted to work. She was trained and ready. And yet she couldn't. For the life of her, Lucy, a Wellesley graduate taught to excel and be anything she wanted, couldn't understand why they wouldn't let her. [20]

Lucy's treatment wasn't an exception by any means. The Agency was grossly underutilizing women during the sixties—and long after, if we're being honest. And it started from the beginning. Whether it was minimizing their experience in their initial interview or not allowing them to jump out of planes like their male classmates during their Farm training, it was clear the women were second-class citizens. Even so, the women held their own, trudging through swamps divided into exact replicas of borders in Europe at the Farm. Whatever you drew, you were given three days to study it at night and figure out how you would traverse the (at times) chest-high waters laden with snakes and God knows what else.[21] And if women accompanied their husbands on an overseas tour, the Agency forced them to resign, rather than leverage capable, competent employees already strategically placed in the field. If women were "lucky," they would be picked up on contract or simply wait to be hired back when they returned to the States at the end of the tour.[22]

Despite female officers' successful completion of training and work as "contract wives," their mostly male managers couldn't imagine a situation in which women could be successful overseas, particularly in cultures and environments where women were considered inferior to men. What these managers didn't realize, however, was that it was this exact reason that women were at an advantage in the field. They could fly under the radar.

Women found that being underestimated worked in their favor—it wouldn't have even occurred to anyone that they were spies, which is the best you can hope for when it comes to espionage. Sue McCloud, a retired CIA officer who was one of six women in her Farm class of about sixty, echoed this in a phone call from her home in Carmel-by-the-Sea, California.

"In a place like [REDACTED], it's very easy to fade into the woodwork because they're not used to seeing women in substantive positions," she explained.

And when women go unnoticed, that's when the magic happens.

"There are more options for what women can do [operationally]," Sue told me. "A woman can get away with murder compared to what the guys do. They [women] were innocuous on the street corner for dead drops or brush passes."[23]

Moreover, women often noticed things in their environment that men didn't. One former operations officer, Patty, attributed it to women being more sensitive to their physical protection, which made them better at identifying surveillants on foot and in stores. Another former operations officer, named Meredith, noted how much nicer the surveillants' socks and shoes were than the locals', which was always a dead giveaway to her.

"That would never occur to my husband to look at," she said.[24] Simply put, women's attention to detail was immensely helpful when it came to operations.

Women also found that targets and recruited assets were sometimes more likely to open up to them than their male counterparts, either because they were oblivious to the possibility of women being spies or because they found women to be more nurturing and appreciated their taking an interest in their personal lives and families.

"I think women are better listeners and better readers of character right off the bat," Sue said. "We have a natural curiosity about people. Men are often trying to see who is going to out-impress the other one."

Not only that, women who were married with children could use that as an entrée to a potential source, she noted. While Sue never married and thus didn't have the opportunity to use that tactic, she says she never considered her choice a sacrifice. In fact, she described it as helpful at times not to be "burdened with children," as she described it. I can't help but wonder if that was also a contributing factor to her serving six successful field tours, including two as chief of station, a rarity for women during her time.[25]

NAME: JANINE BROOKNER
YEAR OF BIRTH: 1940
PLACE OF BIRTH: SYRACUSE, NEW YORK
ENTRANCE ON DUTY: 1968

FIELD TRADECRAFT CERTIFICATION: YES
HOME BASE: SOUTHEAST ASIA
FOREIGN LANGUAGES: TAGALOG, THAI, SPANISH

Like Lucy, Janine craved an adventurous life overseas, but when she began her master's degree at New York University in the mid-sixties, she didn't have any intention of joining the CIA. To her, adventure meant joining the Peace Corps. But when a professor suggested she consider a career in espionage, her path diverted.[26] She joined the Agency shortly after her graduation in 1968. A single mother from Syracuse, New York, Janine was the daughter of a real estate broker mother and a father who worked in newspaper distribution. Her sister, Judy, a shy, quiet artist, was two years her senior; her brother Gary was seven years younger, and after another seven years came Art, her youngest brother. The large age gaps between Janine and her brothers meant she often felt more like an auntie than a sibling.

After her divorce from her first husband, Janine attended NYU and lived in Greenwich Village with her young son, Steven, and a boyfriend named Leo, an eccentric guy who loved working on his MG. Art visited her there often and had a fabulous time. She was a free spirit and a party girl, although she never smoked marijuana, a staple at many parties in the sixties. Art had come to think of Janine as his guardian angel. His father—Janine's stepfather—was abusive, and his mother was too afraid to stick up for him, so it was Janine who did instead.[27]

Janine took that same tenacity with her to the CIA, arriving at headquarters on her first day driving her red Volkswagen Beetle, a fairly popular car in 1968. In fact, there were probably a hundred red VW Beetles in the headquarters parking lot that day, her longtime friend George Amato told me more than fifty years later, and Janine had no idea where she parked her car when she left work that day.[28] The two of them became fast friends after meeting in orientation earlier that morning, and Janine graciously offered to give George a ride back to his temporary housing so that he wouldn't need to take the bus. After walking around the behemoth parking lot for several minutes, which I can tell you didn't become any easier to navigate when I was there decades later, someone took pity on Janine and George and offered to drive them around until they found her car.

Not long after her orientation, Janine and her new friend George began their operational training at the Farm, where she was one of six women in their class of sixty-six—one of even fewer who would go on to become an operations officer in the DO.[29,30]

After graduation, Janine was diagnosed with an atrial septal defect in her heart. Her eldest brother, Gary, was in the military and deployed to Germany at the time, and while on watch one evening in the winter during military maneuvers, he received a phone call on the emergency telephone at an outpost in the middle of the woods. It was Janine. She told him she needed open-heart surgery, and she already arranged a flight for him along with approval for thirty days' leave so that he could be with her through the surgery. Gary remained by her side through the operation, and she continued her recovery at her mother and stepfather's home in Metuchen, New Jersey, where she spent more time with her brother Art.

Upon returning to headquarters, Janine fought for the medical clearance that would allow her to go overseas, which didn't come easily. In fact, there was a period of time in which Janine thought she would never be cleared for an overseas tour due to her heart condition and subsequent surgery. This was an era when women were often put into desk jobs for far less: the mere fear that women would "go off and get married to the next guy"— which was the reason one manager gave Janine for why he'd never hire her.³¹ But by 1969, she prevailed, and the adventure Janine had been hoping for was ready to begin.

The outgoing chief of an East Asia station (COS), George K., was looking for a woman to PCS, short for "Permanent Change of Station," to his station—something he knew wasn't being done anywhere else in the Agency. He was interested in experimenting to see what a female operations officer could do, if given the opportunity. Janine interviewed for the position and got it. She studied the local language at the CIA's language facility in preparation for her tour in East Asia, where she and her son, Steven, who was just six years old at the time, arrived in August 1969.

She was placed in a small office on the ground floor behind the main entrance. There were only three of them in that office—Janine, another operations officer named Colin Thompson, and a secretary. Since the office was small and separate from other Agency components, they had to lock their safes any time they left. It would be another six months before George K. came out as COS, and in the meantime, a man named Horace was the chief. And Horace simply didn't know what to do with Janine.³²,³³,³⁴,³⁵

For the first few months, Horace had her read the local newspapers in English and then brief him periodically on the content, so he'd be up-to-date for country team meetings. But Janine had bigger ambitions for her first tour as an operations officer. There was a large group of expat women, so she joined them and had almost instant access to the young elite. Attractive, blond, five two, and only 110 pounds, Janine was an immediate focus of the local men in the elite group, and that gave her a lot of entrée, which she made good use of. Colin also began bringing Janine along to his meetings with one particular asset who was concerned people might assume he was gay if they saw two men at a restaurant together, which was frowned upon at the time in the country. So the asset, Ben, would bring along his mistress, and Colin started bringing Janine to balance things out, which gave Janine some exposure to more traditional agent handling. When she wasn't reading newspapers for the chief of station, she continued cultivating relationships and writing it all up, only to have Horace ignore her efforts. But her work wouldn't go unnoticed for much longer, as Horace prepared to leave Station and make way for the much more progressive and supportive COS, George.[36,37,38,39]

NAME: MARTHA "MARTI" PETERSON
YEAR OF BIRTH: 1945
PLACE OF BIRTH: KANSAS CITY, MISSOURI
ENTRANCE ON DUTY: 1973
FIELD TRADECRAFT CERTIFICATION: YES
HOME BASE: RUSSIA HOUSE
FOREIGN LANGUAGE: RUSSIAN

At the same time Lucy and Janine were undergoing operational training at the Farm and getting their careers as operations officers off the ground, a woman named Marti was finishing up her bachelor's degree in sociology at Drew University in New Jersey in 1969. Marti grew up in nearby Connecticut, in a family that ascribed to what they considered "traditional gender roles." Her father was a successful businessman, and her mother a homemaker, who, despite her lack of education, found herself busy volunteering and becoming involved in all sorts of activities for which she had no training.

As a result, Marti was raised with the mindset that she could do anything. It was never couched in a negative way, she told me—simply, you are who you are, and the world is yours.

That said, Marti wasn't necessarily intentional about her studies. When she graduated with a bachelor's degree in sociology, she didn't have a plan. So when her father was struggling with alcohol, she moved to Florida to help her family after graduation. She started working for Delta Airlines shortly after, taking reservations and enjoying the travel benefits that came along with the position.[40]

While in college, Marti began dating a man named John Peterson, and after graduation, John had been accepted to three graduate school programs. He wanted to be a writer. Even with those acceptance letters in hand, he felt he needed to go into military service. He believed that writers should have authentic experiences. Marti could understand his reasoning, but admittedly, she wasn't happy with his decision.

"People were getting killed in Vietnam," she told me from her home in North Carolina. But John went through all the training and eventually was deployed to Vietnam for six months. When he came home, he and Marti got married. She assumed the next step would be graduate school for John, but he told her instead that he had already applied to the CIA's paramilitary program. He began training, and Marti went to graduate school at the University of North Carolina for a master's in college teaching. She envisioned herself teaching at a community college, but life had other plans.

"Well, Marti," John said after he finished his training. "We have our first assignment, and it's in Laos."

While few women were breaking into clandestine operations in the sixties, more were becoming reports officers (later called collection management officers, or CMOs), who serve as the link between case officers and the field and headquarters analysts, and even landing in other directorates, where gender discrimination was arguably less prevalent. This was in part because, I've been told, women were thought to be better at research-type roles [than they were at operations]. (One could argue that relegating women to reports work was an example of gender discrimination in and of itself, but nonetheless, there were more women there.) Take Amy Tozzi, for example, whose COS recognized her potential and made her a junior reports officer while on her first tour to Central America in 1961.

"Yes, the DO was a man's world, but in my experience, I was fortunate to have seniors—chief of station and deputy chief of station—who knew an asset when they saw one, and they'd much rather have me doing reports than just sitting there typing stuff," she told me.

Amy was lucky indeed. She had a full-time job in charge of political parties and doing translations. When riots broke out in-country after President Kennedy's assassination, she was on the streets taking photos and filming. She lived at the CIA station for three days and handled all of the reporting.[41]

Debra, who was placed in the Central Reference Service—a position seemingly "more appropriate" for women—didn't experience such excitement from the get-go. She soon found that her position wasn't similar to her experience working at libraries at all. Instead, she was doing reference work for customers, primarily inside the Agency. They held all the biographic files for the CIA and much of the intelligence community. She also wrote biographic profiles on leaders from Latin America, which she told me was incredibly boring.

"Nobody gave a damn," she said.

She worked in a small office space with all women—incredible women who inspired her. One left and became a forest ranger, and one vowed to kill herself at thirty-five because, she said, she'd no longer be beautiful. (When I asked her what ever became of her, she couldn't tell me.) Ultimately, they became ladies doing DI analysis. It became an appealing role for women who were trying to combine a career with any other life interest, including having a family, because it didn't have the same demand as current intelligence or a task force.[42] What Debra didn't know at the time was that she was laying the groundwork for a discipline that would later be called "leadership analysis" and grow to include countless women (including yours truly!) and men over the years and gain the respect of the president and the most senior policymakers.

Meanwhile, in the Directorate of Science and Technology (DS&T), women like Terry were given a unique opportunity to be a part of the Office of Computer Services. After an interview with a charming CIA recruiter, Terry took the IBM programming aptitude test. When she graduated from college in the spring of 1968, she reported for duty at headquarters in August, where IBM employees trained a mix of women and men on the IBM operating system. "I was very lucky because I was starting with the guys. I was friends with all of them. We had male bosses, no women bosses anywhere, but they were great." Terry would go on to become the most senior woman in the DS&T and a member of the Senior Intelligence Service (SIS) ranks, retiring in 1997 as the director of the Office of Information Technology.[43]

The start of the next decade would usher in a new era of opportunities for women. For Marti, that meant a future career of her own at the CIA, but not before experiencing a major personal loss that would turn her world upside down. Lucy would experience a loss of her own, although a different kind, before beginning a productive field tour in which she would face intense discrimination. As for Janine, her star would continue to rise as she found more success as a case officer. For women everywhere—the Agency and beyond—doors were opening, and it seemed all they had to do was choose.[44]

CHAPTER 2

THE SECOND-WAVE SEVENTIES

The women's liberation movement found its way into the mainstream in the seventies as second-wave feminists fought for equality through the Equal Rights Amendment (ERA)—a proposed amendment to the Constitution to protect equal rights under law regardless of sex—and found inspiration from women like Gloria Steinem; Kate Millett, author of *Sexual Politics*; and Susan Brownmiller, author of *Against Our Will: Men, Women, and Rape*. In 1973, the Supreme Court's landmark decision in *Roe v. Wade*, protecting a pregnant person's right to have an abortion, was considered a watershed moment for women's rights. Indeed, the women's movement had made such an impact that *Time* magazine even named "American women" as its "Man of the Year" in 1975, noting that they were "not quite the same subordinate creatures they were before."[1]

And while feminist icon Steinem may have criticized New York's Playboy Club in *Show* magazine the decade prior, some women—including *another* Gloria—viewed it as a place full of opportunity.[2] Gloria Hendry of Bond Girl fame has credited her time there as a Playboy Bunny for launching her acting career. When she received the call that the Bond franchise was interested in casting her as a Bond Girl opposite Roger Moore in the 1973 film *Live and Let Die*, she thought it was a mistake.

"No way. I'm not tall, I'm not blond, I don't have big breasts. Why do they want to see me?" Hendry asked.

But it wasn't a mistake. Hendry became Bond's first Black romantic partner. Women of color at the CIA, however, were few and far between.

"I used to walk around at lunch looking for another brown person who wasn't secretarial or logistics," Carmen Medina, a former CIA analyst and coauthor of *Rebels at Work*, told me. She was keenly aware of her identity as both a woman and a Puerto Rican when she entered on duty toward the end of the decade in 1978. It seemed that despite some of the progress for women on the outside, the environment continued to be quite limited for women at the Agency, and even more so for women of color. Carmen noted that many of the young women the Agency began hiring were placed in the operations center, which was evenly split between men and women at the time.[3]

Drinking was a part of the culture then, Carmen told me (I can confirm this was still true thirty years later), and that meant lunch was a time for the old boys to throw back some beers. Carmen recounted the first time she was invited to join them.

"I knew in my mind this was an important invitation . . . that I shouldn't blow it," she said.

It was clear to her that there was an unspoken expectation: In order to succeed, she'd need to do what the men did, even as an analyst in the DI.[4] But for Carmen, unlike some other women, that didn't include changing her personality, as she found that her natural way of being happened to be compatible with male-ordered organizations, which she said worked to her advantage.

Meanwhile, in the DO, women were still trying to prove they had what it takes to recruit and handle assets. It wasn't until 1979 that the CIA hired women fully as case officers right off the bat; previously they were brought in under some other wrapper, like a reports officer. But now, a year after the Civil Service Reform Act, which required the "the recruitment of a representative work-force,"[5] the Agency complied and hired more women, including into case officer roles, even if it did so while kicking and scream-ing. A woman named Margery* was part of that first class that included women case officers, and when she stood up to give a presentation, one of her male classmates shouted, "You're only here because they had to start hiring women!"

Without missing a beat, Margery looked him dead in the eye and said, "I'm here because I'm so goddamn good."[6] Born with only one arm and having used a prosthesis at a young age, Mar-gery didn't suffer bullies. Besides, she knew she was there because she was qualified. Despite having a father who didn't believe in funding women's education, Margery took her inspiration from her well-educated mother, one of the few in her generation who had both a bachelor's and master's degree. Margery, for her part, had a bachelor's degree in European history and fine arts and a master's degree in education.[7] But she wasn't the only skilled woman at the CIA in the seventies; women like Marti, Lucy, and Janine were already making waves before Margery arrived.

Marti

Like many women at the CIA in the seventies, Marti began her career as a "CIA wife," providing secretarial and administrative support to Station. When her husband, John, told her they were going to Laos, her plans for becoming a teacher were diverted, and before she knew it, she wasn't just *living* in Southeast Asia. Marti, too, was working for the CIA. The Agency saw in the wives an opportunity for good, cheap labor. As a bonus, it kept them from spending the days blending daquiris at each other's homes—their go-to activity in Laos. After all, there wasn't much else to do. There was no way out of Pakse except by plane. No television, no radio, no phone calls, no newspapers, and mail only occasionally. Marti felt she had a pretty good setup, but even so, she despised working as a clerk.

"I always felt like, you know, I'm not stupid. And here I was, doing filing, typing, wrapping the pouch," she told me. She knew she was smarter and had accomplished more than many of the men she worked for.[8] But it seemed it didn't matter how well educated she was or that she had prior work experience. The spouses were there to type and provide whatever secretarial support Station (read: men) needed. She was growing increasingly frustrated with the mundane work and the lack of intellectual stimulation, so she began an application to the Fulbright scholarship program. However, she soon learned CIA employees couldn't be associated with Fulbright. (This separation policy remains even today in order to protect the integrity of the Fulbright program and other humanitarian programs like the US Peace Corps.) Marti tore up her application, and after a while, she got used to her routine in Laos.

"It was hard to be just John's wife. I was lost without my own identity. I struggled in the office doing the lowest, mindless jobs. . . . John did not treat me this way, but we had so little time together. I learned to swallow my pride and accept that I was an appendage to his career," she wrote in her memoir, *Widow Spy*.[9]

The officers and their wives sustained themselves watching movies as a group and enjoyed what Marti described as a "pretty simple life."

But everything changed fifteen months later, when the chief of their office showed up at Marti's door one October evening in 1972.

"Marti," he said. "It's John. He's gone." John's closest friend Leon came, and with tears running down his face, explained to Marti that John's helicopter had been shot down.

Marti and John's time in Pakse was part of the CIA's covert war in Laos to take control from the Communist Pathet Lao, a group allied with North Vietnam and the Soviet Union during the Vietnam War, a plan that was initiated in 1961 just before President Dwight D. Eisenhower left office. Eisenhower believed that "if Laos were lost, the rest of Southeast Asia would follow." By 1962, a secret war began, which included escalated air support to guerrilla fighters.[10] In 1971, John became a direct part of that plan, serving as a paramilitary officer, training Lao troops deployed into the jungle to interdict the North Vietnamese Army troops' march to South Vietnam and disrupt Communist supply routes across the Ho Chi Minh Trail to Vietnam.[11,12] By 1973, Laos had become the most bombed country per capita in the world, with more than two million tons of bombs dropped over the country over a nine-year period. An estimated 728 Americans died in Laos, including CIA officers.[13,14]

When I visited headquarters in mid-2023, I took a few minutes to pay my respects to the fallen officers at the CIA Officers Memorial Wall. I scanned the open book encased in glass just below the stars until my eyes landed on the name of John Peterson, and I reflected on my conversation with Marti about the day she lost him.

"The day he was killed, his life came to an end as mine did too. I had no way forward," she told me. I could still see the grief on her face, even some fifty years later. And so, after the funeral, Marti went home to Florida, where she spent time sitting. She tried to figure out a way to move forward without him. She was only twenty-seven years old and deep in loss and grief. Two months later, she went to Washington and stayed with some friends, who suggested she embark on a true CIA career herself. She thought, *Well, that sounds as good as anything.* After all, it wouldn't be her first time doing work for the CIA. Her friend Glen set up an interview for her, which Marti assumed would be with the Career Trainee program, but instead, it was a recruiter at the Ames building in Rosslyn, Virginia. The interview went well, and at the end, the recruiter said he had several secretary positions for her. That wasn't what Marti wanted nor who she was. She politely left and called Glen.

"This isn't what I want to do," she told him. "I have qualifications. This is not what I want." The reality, however, was that women were largely hired as clericals at that point. Marti didn't consider it a "fight"; that was just the way it was. Typing, filing, teaching, nursing, mothering—those were the skills women were *supposed* to have. But Marti had already been working for the Agency and was highly educated. She knew she was capable of much more. With that in mind, Glen went back to the drawing board and eventually set up an interview for Marti with the Career Trainee program.

A year after her husband's death, Marti joined the CIA as a full-time employee—not in the secretarial role they initially offered her but as one of only four women in what was now called the Career Trainee (CT) class. In her first recruitment scenario, her instructor, who was pretending to be a potential intelligence asset, was a rather abrupt man. The two went into a room for the meeting, where they were filmed. He was sitting on one end of the sofa, and Marti was on the other. She developed rapport with him, as she was taught to do, and as she moved the conversation toward her recruitment pitch, he inched more and more toward the edge of the sofa. By the end of the pitch, he was basically hanging on to the end of the sofa, not looking at her, visibly very uncomfortable at the idea of a woman recruiting him, even in a fictitious scenario.

Marti found it even more amusing to see it replayed on film. "It was a classic moment in training," she told me.

Marti got through her training with ease, and when she returned to headquarters, the hunt began for an assignment. She knew she wanted to go overseas and do operations, but she didn't have a particular area she was aspiring to serve in—certainly not Moscow. She didn't speak Russian, but she spoke Spanish and performed well on her Modern Language Aptitude Test (MLAT), which meant she could learn foreign languages fairly well. She was first offered a position in Burma as an intelligence assistant, now called a staff operations officer (SOO) or desk officer. When she turned that down, she was offered another similar position domestically, and again, she turned it down. Marti didn't want to sit at a desk and do name traces, one of the primary functions of a desk officer—necessary work, but at times terribly boring. She wanted to run operations in the field.

"I told them, 'I don't think so,'" she said. "That was ballsy." That would have been ballsy even in today's climate, let alone during a time when very few women were offered field tours, period. Soon after, Marti had an interview with a man for an opportunity she never would have predicted.

"I've read your file, and I see you did very well in training," he told her. "You have good language skills. We think you may do well in a denied area. You've been through a lot of stress losing your husband."

Marti listened to him intently.

"I think we could make you part of our team going to Moscow."

She was shocked. A tour in the Soviet Union wasn't something she had thought of, let alone been gunning for. She was a junior officer straight out of the Farm, for Pete's sake, she said. And so, Marti spent a year learning Russian in preparation for a tour in Moscow. She experienced an incredible bias from the instructors, who were all from St. Petersburg before it was Leningrad. Since they didn't tell them what positions the students were filling, the instructors assumed Marti was a spouse and that all she really needed to learn was grocery vocabulary, prompting her to course correct them several times. "No, I'm really going to be working at the embassy," she'd tell them. When she finished language school each day, Marti unwound by driving to tae kwon do class in Manassas, Virginia, all the while listening to her Russian cassette tapes in the car.

After language training, Marti went through the Agency's Internal Operations Course, required training for denied areas, in which she would learn to conduct covert operations, including the art of dead drops, car tosses, signals, and asset meetings. She also took the advanced surveillance detection course, all with an eye of preparing her for operating in one of the most hostile counterintelligence environments in the world.

By July 1975, the other officers and their wives with whom Marti had been through training (at the time wives were given surveillance detection and language training along with Agency-paid babysitters to watch their children while they did it!) deployed to Moscow. Due to some delays in adding a slot for her, Marti didn't arrive in Moscow for another four months. And when she did, she wasn't met by anyone from Station, of course. She was a new officer in a new position without a history. She had a clean slate—a perfect scenario when traveling to a denied area as a CIA officer because the KGB would have no reason to suspect her.

Marti arrived at the embassy and told the Marine guard that she was a new arrival and gave him the name of her section.

The guard called down to the secretary and office manager, a woman named Kate, who was expecting her. After meeting everyone in the office for her cover job, Kate then took Marti down to Station, which was essentially a metal box. Marti went inside, where everyone she knew from back in Washington was waiting. She was both thrilled and relieved to see those familiar faces from training.

"You know, Marti," the COS began. "This is the only place you can know us."

Marti knew it was essential to her cover that she not associate with anyone from Station unless there was a visible way to connect her to them. Her cover, above all else, was important. Marti began meeting people at the Marine house and living the perceived life of a single woman in Moscow. She hiked with girlfriends and even learned to cross-country ski, mail-ordering a set of skis from a store in Helsinki. When she was out, she wore her SRR-100, a receiver strapped to her bra with a new type of Velcro that enabled her to listen to the KGB's unencrypted radio transmissions to determine whether they were following her throughout Moscow.

Hours, days, and weeks went by, and Marti still hadn't detected surveillance. She was confident that she had traveled to enough places, including remote areas, in an effort to draw out surveillance, to confirm she wasn't being followed. It seemed to her that the KGB didn't find a group of women on various excursions worth their time. Their chauvinism worked in Marti's (and Station's) favor. Even so, Station wasn't entirely convinced. Surely, she wasn't seeing them, right? They decided to test Marti's skills by positioning another officer, Mike, and his wife at a currency store along her route that gave him full view of her tangerine Zhiguli as she drove by. Just as Marti anticipated, Mike didn't see surveillance, nor did he hear broadcasts over the KGB's radio frequency that would indicate she was being followed. He reported back to Station that Marti was indeed surveillance-free or "black."

The office was satisfied, at least for now, but doubts in Marti's ability to spot surveillance remained. In some respects this was understandable, given that they were operating in a denied area—you can never be too careful—but one can't help but wonder if some of those doubts were linked to her being a first tour officer, and more importantly, a woman. At any rate, Marti said such doubts prompted her to remain vigilant, which is never a bad idea, particularly in such a high-risk country.

Once it was determined that Marti could identify surveillance, the chief selected her to serve as a backup in the event the deputy chief, Jack, could not pick up a package from Station's most prized asset, a man named Aleksandr Ogorodnik, code-named TRIGON. TRIGON was recruited in January 1973 while serving a tour in the Soviet Embassy in Bogotá. He was a prolific reporter who quickly proved his worth to Station, offering unique insight into Soviet relations in Latin America. TRIGON considered defecting and staying abroad, but after some coaxing from his case officer, the lure of more financial gain, and the idea of changing the system from within, he opted to return to Moscow in hopes of gaining a position in the government that would give him even greater access to information of interest to the United States.

It took several months for TRIGON to make contact after he arrived in Moscow in late fall 1974. Station had given him instructions to wait three months before signaling, as it was standard for the KGB to put returning diplomats through intense investigations to ensure they hadn't been recruited by a foreign intelligence service while serving abroad. When February came, TRIGON did not signal. In fact, it was several months before he parked his vehicle at a signal site code-named PARK-PLATZ as agreed to in the communication plan before he left

Bogotá. It was only a month into Marti's time in Moscow when she was pulled into the case.

Jack successfully picked up the first package from TRIGON while on his regular jogging route. Hidden in a flattened milk carton was a secret message from the asset, which noted he had secured a position in the Global Affairs Department in the Ministry of Foreign Affairs, providing incredible access to classified cables coming in and out of Soviet embassies around the world.[15,16]

In his next package, TRIGON provided photographs of nearly one hundred secret Soviet government documents, disguised in a dirty rag soaked in diesel oil. In this message, he reminded Station of the promise his case officer had made to him back in Bogotá when he agreed to return to Moscow—that headquarters would consider providing him with an L-pill, or poison. Knowing the risk he was putting himself in by committing treason within the borders of the Soviet Union, TRIGON wanted to be prepared to take his own life if he were arrested by the KGB. Although it sounds like something straight out of a spy novel, this is not standard procedure for the CIA, and the handling officer, along with headquarters, was wary of giving an asset a suicide pill. In fact, both Bogotá Station and headquarters were unanimous in their disapproval. They considered it immoral and unethical. At the same time, they had come to know and respect TRIGON and found it difficult not to at least consider giving him control over his future.[17,18] And so, after some more thought, the handling officer agreed to present TRIGON's case to headquarters.

Several months passed before the next package drop for TRIGON, during which time Marti continued to live her cover as single "Party Marti." She also had a budding romance with the embassy communicator, a man named Steve whose wife had gone home to the States. Marti wasn't interested at first—a married man wasn't an area where she was interested in venturing. Besides, she had met his wife before she returned to the States and really liked her. Marti found her helpful and kind. But as she and Steve got to know each other, laughing over beers at the Marine house, they grew closer. And their relationship became one of the many secrets Marti kept while serving in Moscow, although this one wouldn't prove to be as dangerous as others.

After some practice runs at headquarters, Station became concerned that a car toss could damage the miniature camera inside the next package for TRIGON, which meant an officer would have to make the delivery on foot. Since Marti still didn't have surveillance on her, she was the most logical person for this dead drop. More time passed, and it wasn't until April that Marti made her inaugural drop for TRIGON. She left her apartment feeling nervous yet confident about the delivery, knowing she had spent months learning the city inside and out. She made her way through Soviet neighborhoods and remote industrial areas. She became more provocative in her route, taking multiple trains to flush out surveillance. But no one was following her. When she arrived at the drop site, she leaned on the snowbank, pretended to adjust her boot, and gently placed the crumpled cigarette package on the snowy ground. She returned an hour and a half later only to find TRIGON had not retrieved the package. Disappointed, she recovered it and traveled back to the embassy Marine bar, where another CIA officer confirmed her safe return.

Station brainstormed possible explanations for why TRIGON was a no-show, but it was difficult for them to know for sure. With no future delivery dates scheduled, they went back to the original plan of looking for TRIGON's car parked at the signal site, PARKPLATZ. And when they finally saw it a month later, Marti was again selected to deliver the package—this time straight through his car window as the deputy chief had done months prior. Although Marti's first delivery to TRIGON hadn't gone as planned, this one went off without a hitch.

With contact reestablished and future delivery dates secured, Station was ready to deliver on its promise. Both headquarters and Station were now in agreement that it was their "moral obligation" to provide TRIGON with the L-pill, and with the proper approvals in place, it was time for Station to decide who would deliver the poison, disguised in a fountain pen, similar to the one with the miniature camera they had already given him. A sure sign of Station's confidence in her, Marti was chosen to deliver the most important package to TRIGON. Marti tucked the package, disguised as a small log, into her waistband, holding it close to her body while twisting and turning through Moscow on a well-lit summer evening. She was relieved to see that the drop site offered some shadows for cover as she placed it near the lamppost. When she returned later, it was gone, and in its place, a crushed milk carton with intelligence from TRIGON.

The KGB continued to ignore Marti, and so she continued to conduct deliveries to TRIGON surveillance-free, as did a handful of other experienced officers. What followed were regular timed exchanges often at the same drop site during the same clandestine outing, including the delivery of another L-pill after TRIGON destroyed the first one out of caution when his office was under suspicion. Station opted to reuse sites, even though they were advised against doing this in training, because they thought it was better than risking TRIGON not finding a package in a new location.

After some time, Station began to notice anomalies in TRIGON's reporting. The quality of his photographs was deteriorating, as was his health. They started to consider that he may be under KGB control. When it came time for the next drop, Marti was uneasy and even suggested another officer conduct the drop since her tour would end in just a few months. She knew that didn't make sense though—she was the only officer who had delivered to that particular site, and if she were arrested, it wouldn't be a significant blow to Station's numbers, as her replacement would be arriving soon enough. Despite the anomalies in TRIGON's reporting and the suspicions over whether it was in fact him who drew the red signal on the agreed upon location, the new chief of station, Gene, wasn't about to admit his doubts to headquarters. The op would move forward, but this time, Marti wasn't alone when she arrived at the location. She made her way up the stairs of the bridge to the pedestrian walkway and placed the package, but before she made it all the way back down, three men approached rapidly and grabbed her. They ripped open her blouse, revealing the SRR-100. Kicking and screaming, she explained she was American and gave the number for the US Embassy as a van pulled up and flung open the doors, revealing ten to twenty more men.

Marti had been caught.

She was transported to Lubyanka prison, where she was interrogated until the KGB finally called the consular chief, Cliff, from the US Embassy, who arrived and corroborated her story. It became clear to Marti that she was ambushed, and TRIGON had been apprehended. After several hours of questioning and even an attempt at coercing her into confessing to espionage, the KGB released Marti. She returned to Station, where her colleagues and new chief were awaiting her, along with a message Gene had written on the board: "Welcome back, our little girl!" It seemed that regardless of the many difficult nights Marti had traversed the cold, lonely streets of Moscow and the seamless dead drops and timed exchanges she had successfully accomplished, it wasn't enough to gain the respect of her new chief, who insisted that Marti had inadvertently brought surveillance to the drop site.

That accusation would haunt Marti for seven years after she was expelled from Moscow until the Agency would confirm that TRIGON had been compromised by double agents, Karl and Hana Koecher, working for the Czech intelligence service and the CIA. As part of Karl Koecher's CIA contract in Virginia, he translated telephone taps recorded in Bogotá when TRIGON was serving there. When the couple was arrested in 1984 for providing intelligence to the Czech service and the KGB, the Agency finally learned the full details of TRIGON's arrest, in which he sealed his own fate with the L-pill Marti had delivered. She could finally rest easy knowing that it was nothing she did, or didn't do, that led to the arrest of Station's most important Moscow asset, who had become both a friend to the Agency and a hero.

Lucy

At the same time Marti was navigating her way at the Agency and in Moscow as a widow spy, Lucy was finding her place in a world before tandem CIA couples existed. Much to her relief, she didn't go to Africa as a housewife with her case officer husband as planned. After several offers for postings overseas, he was finally offered a position in Washington, which allowed Lucy to continue to work at headquarters. She switched from China ops to Covert Action. It was clear that now that she was married, she wouldn't be going overseas, and certainly not to China. She also suffered from a severe case of mononucleosis—initially misdiagnosed as Hodgkin's disease—which only further complicated her ability to deploy. And so, she ran a large international book program involving literature around the world as a part of the Agency's covert action initiatives.

While Lucy enjoyed the covert action work, she was starting to feel like she was losing herself in an effort to be the perfect wife. One night just before her birthday, her husband came home and said, "I got my two identities mixed up and got involved with my agent." He was having an affair. It was like a knife in Lucy's heart. She was devastated. Not long after, she heard the woman was pregnant. While it was all very shocking to Lucy, she learned it wasn't news to everyone else. "We all knew it was happening," a colleague told her.

Heartbroken as she may have been after the divorce, Lucy had to plan her next career move. Capitol Hill was now investigating the CIA's involvement in stunt labor movements, and they started cutting back the Agency's covert action programs as a result of the Church Committee. A friend of hers was in Europe Division (EUR), and Lucy began to think that would be a better fit. She knew French and Spanish, after all. She interviewed for an ops officer position in EUR but learned they had no interest in taking additional women.

"We already have a woman we like," the hiring manager told her. A common refrain of the time—so long as there was one female, that was more than enough. Lucy was given a desk job in EUR instead. *I'm going to be the little old lady in tennis shoes*, she thought to herself, when all she really wanted was to be in the field meeting assets. The writing was on the wall. If she stayed in this position, it was a dead end. After some finagling, Lucy landed a field tour in a sensitive undisclosed location. It wasn't her first pick though—she wanted to go to New York more than anything. She thought it was attainable because it was so difficult to get officers to serve in a location with such a high cost of living. But the chief there had strong opinions about female operations officers.

"Lucy, you're going to spend your time shopping," he told her. And even more insulting: "I really don't think you can talk to big-deal men."

It turns out she could. Lucy was outproducing the male officers in her current Station, but even so, when it came time for promotion, she was passed over. Her COS told her not to worry. She'd get it next time. He assumed she was upset. But it didn't dawn on her to be upset. She was so used to being overlooked by this point. Not to mention the unwanted advances. The deputy chief of station (DCOS) made a habit of running his fingers up her rib cage. On one particular occasion, she was wearing open-toed shoes when presenting what she thought was a brilliant piece on the Organization of the Petroleum Exporting Countries. Instead of being impressed by her report, her DCOS was enamored with her feet.

"Your toes really turn me on," he told her. When Lucy told her COS about it and how uncomfortable it made her feel, *he* came onto her as well. He told her his wife was a lesbian and pleaded with Lucy to go away with him.

"I'm sure I never said, 'You disgusting pig,'" Lucy told me decades later from her home in Manhattan. Instead, she gently told him that although he was wonderful, she couldn't get involved with him because he was her boss. "You just tried to make sure that, whatever happened, the man's ego was not damaged, and you retained good relations. Especially if he was your boss." I nodded knowingly, feeling even more of a kinship with her than I already had. It seems even four decades wasn't enough time to change some things at the Agency.[19,20]

There were two offices in the station where Lucy was posted, but she always had her eye on the operational side. She met a successful (married) businessman who agreed to introduce her to a very high-level businessman in New York. Lucy got approval to TDY—meaning temporary duty assignment—to New York with her contact, who would serve as a conduit to the target. Her contact was staying in a fancy hotel in Greenwich Village, nothing like the dump the Agency had booked for her stay.

"I remember thinking, *Thank God he's not staying in my hotel because it was anything but James Bond*," Lucy told me.

The two of us laughed—if people only knew how unlike James Bond the Agency really is.

Lucy got a call from her contact around midnight, asking her to come to his hotel.

"I need to see you right away," he told her. She walked over in the dark—she wasn't scared or concerned about her safety. She was a trained CIA operations officer, after all. When she arrived, the contact took her to a strip club he owned.

"You look at the show; I've seen it before," he said to Lucy as nude women danced around them. And then, even more concerning, "Listen, the guy doesn't want to meet anymore."

Lucy started to panic. *Oh, my God, my whole op is failing,* she thought to herself.

"Well, we gotta find a way," she told him. She then took her contact back to her grimy hotel and got him set up in a room there. James Bond or not, he was going to have to stay there for the night so they could go to the meeting together in the morning—just a few hours away at this point.

"I'm not staying here alone. If you sleep with me, I'll stay," he said. Then Lucy got stern with him. Under no circumstances would she stay with him. The next morning, after spending the night in her separate room, away from her contact, she went downstairs to meet the target on her own. He would be wearing a trench coat and holding a copy of *The New York Times,* which, as it turned out, wasn't specific enough. Several men approached her, and she even thought one was her target until it became clear that these men thought she was a prostitute. That's the kind of hotel it was.

Lucy returned to her contact's room to find him stark naked when he answered the door. He tried to get her to come inside, but she insisted he come down to join the meeting with her. He eventually did, and Lucy successfully pulled off the ops meeting despite her contact's conduct.

Following the meeting, Lucy met with the chief of another office, who was impressed with the way she handled the men in that meeting. He told her he'd find her a better place to stay and set her up in an Agency safehouse. The safehouses were all named after women at the time, and this particular one, Lucy told me, was called Nancy. The Agency was naming the secretive locations where it met its most sensitive cases after women. I couldn't help but wonder, was this because on some subconscious level women made them feel safe? Or was it because safehouse were objects, just as women were in their eyes?

While Marti and Lucy were busy learning what it meant to be female case officers, other women at the Agency were finding success in, and even creating, different career tracks. Remember Amy whose COS saw potential in her and made her a junior reports officer in Central America in the early sixties? By the seventies, Amy had another tour under her belt, except this time it was in Europe, and she had successfully completed the field tradecraft certification training course at the Farm. Getting in wasn't a walk in the park though, having faced scrutiny during her interview over whether she'd be worth the investment.

"Amy, how do we know you're not just going to go down there to find a husband?" they asked her, point-blank.

"You don't. But I've already served five years, and I think I've shown what I can do, so it's up to you guys." And with that, she got into the program as one of very few women at that time. Once ops-certified, Amy returned to the field, again in Latin America, serving as a linchpin for Station as the only reports officer. She credits much of her success to her COS, Tom, who noted in one of her performance reviews, "If she wore pants, she'd already be a thirteen," meaning if she were a man, she would have been promoted sooner.

"I broke some barriers thanks to Tom," Amy told me. When she returned to headquarters as a GS-13, she became the chief of reports for a Caribbean country and, soon after, chief of reports for Latin America, during which time she created a formal career track for reports officers.

"They realized I wasn't a GS-15. I had just become a 14. To put somebody in [that role] who was at least up to the grade, especially a woman . . . I was very fortunate. I had some very open-minded, asset-oriented supervisors."[21]

Similarly, some women found supportive management in the DI. Katherine Layton, for example, became a branch chief at a time when few women were assigned those positions.[22] While certainly not perfect, it seems that by the seventies, the DI was beginning to set the standard at the Agency for gender equality in the workplace, although there was arguably still a long way to go. When Debra, from the Central Reference Service, was accepted into Johns Hopkins School of Advanced International Studies master's program and requested financial support and a leave of absence from the Agency, her division chief asked her when she'd have another baby.

"I am humiliated to tell you that it didn't dawn on me until years later . . . what had happened. I was denied because I was a woman of childbearing age," she told me.[23]

By and large though, women in the DI had a much more positive experience at this time than those in other parts of the organization. "I didn't feel that gender discrimination in the DI. You really were advanced on the basis of your qualifications. What were you producing? What impact was it having?" Sharon Basso, a retired CIA analyst who spent her first ten years as a secretary before becoming an analyst, told me as she reflected on her career. She began at the Agency in 1964 as a GS-4 and retired as a SIS-3 in 1988.[24,25]

Women in the DO like Janine, however, were still very much locked in battle against gender discrimination.

Janine

When Janine explained to her new COS George K. what she had been doing and the contacts she had made during her first six months in East Asia, he practically fell out of his chair. It was clear to him that Janine had made significant progress, despite the previous chief paying her no attention. The COS brought her there for a purpose, and she was already doing what he hoped a woman case officer could do—find success as a case officer in an environment where people thought only males could be successful.

The predominant opinion among the male case officers in that Station, or frankly, any CIA station at that time, was that the only way a woman could get somewhere in espionage was if she slept with someone. They found it difficult to believe that a woman could recruit a man without having something sexual involved. It was particularly hard for them to stomach when Janine successfully recruited a target whom two other male case officers had attempted but failed to recruit. She truly hit her stride when the deputy chief of station, who didn't appreciate her work, departed—at which point Colin became acting deputy, handing over some of his cases to Janine. [26,27,28,29]

Two years into the tour, Colin's wife returned to the States. Of course, rumors of an affair had already been swirling about the embassy, given the proximity in which Janine and Colin worked. And indeed, working so closely did bring them closer, which only added to the fact that he felt getting married had been a mistake. But it wasn't until after his wife left short of tour that he and Janine got together. Up until then, they were just good friends, although a romantic relationship was bubbling under the surface, just waiting for its chance to come up for air.

As her time in Station wound down, Janine sent her son, Steven, back to the States with a child from the embassy, carrying little plastic containers of water with tropical fish all the way to Janine's mother in New York. Soon after, Janine and Colin departed and traveled through Europe together before returning to the States. They stopped in Beirut and enjoyed a few days in the city, taking pleasure in the little things in life. The seventy-degree climate was a welcome change from the tropical, balmy ninety-five-degree weather they had grown accustomed to.[30]

Janine came out of her East Asia assignment with a fantastic reputation—she made some significant recruitments and had done some noteworthy developmental work. Ann Donohue took Janine's place when her tour ended in 1972. "I've always said, it's better to follow a bad act. Following Janine was impossible because she was incredible," ninety-one-year-old Ann told me over the phone from her home in Washington, DC. "She really had a handle on what was going on, and the agents I inherited from her were top drawer, terrific."[31]

When they returned to headquarters, Janine and Colin were faced with the fact that tandem couples were still rare at this point. And to complicate matters further, they weren't yet married. Colin needed to divorce his first wife.[32] While they sorted out their next tour and personal situation, Janine caught up with old friends, like George Amato from her orientation class, who had also just finished a tour in East Asia. Janine had maintained their friendship and also made new friends at headquarters, including a woman named Susan.[33] Soon after, Janine introduced Susan to George over dinner at a local restaurant called Chez Francois—and the two of them married just six months later.

George had been slated for a tour in South America, but it was deemed too dangerous for a new bride, so they changed it to a more stable country in the same region. Susan, a Chinese American who grew up in Portland, Oregon, was trained privately at a safehouse and sent to language school for three months to learn Spanish. She loved languages, she told me, and getting paid to study a foreign language was a dream come true for her. When the three months were up, Susan and George left for their new post with the promise of Susan becoming a contractor. But when she first arrived, she found there wasn't much work for her, and the work she was doing was unpaid. Susan made connections with the locals who Station suspected were involved in the drug trade, but admittedly, it wasn't the best use of her talents. When a man named Joe Fernandez—who would later become known for his role in the Iran-Contra Affair—found out Susan was working for free, he made sure she got a contract and was paid for her work. Joe told Susan they were interested in Chinese targets and gave her some names to go after. With those names in hand, Susan leveraged her Chinese background and Mandarin-language skills to make inroads to the Chinese Embassy community.[34]

At the same time Susan and George were beginning their new life together as a married couple abroad, Janine and Colin were both offered jobs in Bangkok. (They assumed their old chief, George K., had something to do with it.) Colin went out first in the spring of 1973, and Janine and her son, Steven, followed in July. By September, they were married, but not without substantial persuasion on Colin's part. Janine was reluctant because of her previous marriage, but she felt her son needed a father figure. (Colin admitted to me decades later that he can't say he did a particularly good job at that.) The large wedding ceremony took place in a hotel, complete with carved ice swans, bursting with expats and Station officers, some who were already there and some newly arrived. The hotel was so happy to host an American wedding that they didn't charge a fee.[35]

The environment in Bangkok Station was drastically different from their previous post: too many Americans and not enough work to do. Even so, Janine made some successful recruitments.[36] She was protective of her accomplishments and wasn't always happy about sharing a similar career with Colin. The two of them did some joint operations, but Janine preferred to carve out her own achievements, separate from her husband. That's not to say they didn't help each other. Colin became Station's point person for Soviet targets. Most Agency officers didn't bother; they'd rather find something easier to do. But Colin, together with Janine, entertained the diplomatic community, including the Soviets, at their large home with a swimming pool—they had two housing allowances, after all. During this time, they also adopted a three-year-old Thai girl named Tam.[37]

When Saigon fell in 1975, effectively ending the Vietnam War, some of the people who had been in Cambodia were evacuated to Bangkok, and others from Vietnam came over because they had family there. Everyone, Colin said, was essentially sitting around until they could figure out what to do with them, making for unhappy Station officers—including him. By this time, he had spent the better part of fourteen years working in Southeast Asia—Vietnam, Laos, Bangkok—and when the war ended, he wasn't happy.[38]

That unhappiness took a toll on his marriage to Janine. When they returned to headquarters in 1975, Colin wasn't anxious to go overseas again. Janine, on the other hand, was still her ambitious self and wanted to continue to climb the ladder of success. The two of them separated in 1978 and divorced in

1979, just before Janine departed for a tour in South America with their daughter, Tam, and her son, Steven.[39]

Marti

While Janine was divorcing and preparing for her next tour, Marti was doing the opposite. In mid-June 1978 when news broke of her arrest in Moscow, she was already back at headquarters, having been declared persona non grata by the Soviets after her arrest the previous year. She received a heads-up that Reuters had the story, and when it hit the newswire, she came home to find journalists waiting for her. She avoided them by entering her home through her garage. Her phone was ringing off the hook that night—more reporters requesting to talk to Martha Peterson.

"Not here. I don't know her," Marti told them. She was on the nightly news on all major channels, her picture plastered across the screen. "What do you tell your neighbors? It was bizarre," she said to me, recounting the day her secret was exposed to the world. Thankfully, she had already told Steve about it when she visited him in his station earlier that year, so seeing it in the news didn't come as a surprise to him.

When he finished his tour and divorced his wife, he and Marti married on Thanksgiving Day 1978 in a basement in Fairfax County with only her parents as witnesses. The following year, Marti became pregnant, and they made the decision not to take their kids overseas. And so, she began a new chapter in counterintelligence at headquarters.

Whereas men often lead with their war stories, Marti shied away from talking about her experiences in Moscow. Indeed, much of Marti's life has been cloaked in secrecy—her own children didn't know about her first marriage to John or that she worked for the CIA until they were in high school. Another thirty-plus years would pass before she would finally share her story in her memoir, *The Widow Spy*, and begin speaking publicly about her CIA career.

Despite some of the career highs (and lows) women experienced, overall morale at the Agency had tanked by the end of the seventies. And not just for women. Officers were feeling it across the board. Much of that was due to CIA director Admiral Stansfield Turner's abrupt firing of about two hundred middle-grade and senior DO officers on October 31, 1977, dubbed the "Halloween Massacre," plunging the Agency into turmoil.[40] Janine's friends George and Susan were affected by these cuts, shocked to learn they were let go on the heels of their successful tours in South America.[41] Marti, Lucy, and Janine, however, remained along with plenty of other new recruits who were ready to shake things up.

CHAPTER 3

THE EMPOWERING EIGHTIES

From Madonna's chart-topping "Like a Virgin" to the steep increase of women in the labor force, the eighties saw some important developments for women. Sandra Day O'Connor became the first woman on the US Supreme Court; Sally Ride, the first American woman to fly in space; and Oprah Winfrey, the first woman to produce her own talk show.[1] The decade also included some setbacks—one of the most notable being the failure of the Equal Rights Amendment.

As for the Bond franchise, it debuted its first female protagonist—although the choice to name the character "Octopussy" suggests there was still a long way to go before the objectification of the Bond Girl would end.

At the CIA, the number of female officers had increased by the eighties, and the DI in particular had progressed quite a bit, Carmen Medina told me. There were four women team chiefs and a critical mass of women in Africa Division, where Carmen worked. The DO, on the other hand, was a different story. By this time, the Agency had begun multicultural courses, and Carmen, a Puerto Rican woman, found herself speaking up not just for herself but on behalf of others. She was particularly struck when the male instructors asked a question that required people to admit there was gender or ethnic discrimination. Carmen looked over to Nancy, the chief of Africa Reports, and Nancy didn't say a word. She didn't raise her hand. And so, Carmen raised hers instead.[2]

"We all know that the women in the DO are in reports," said Carmen, who describes herself as irreverent and direct. It was true that even though the number of women had increased in the DO, the penchant for placing them in reports roles rather than in case officer roles continued.[3]

"It demonstrated the power the DO had," Carmen told me decades later. "That when asked a direct question, women would pretend everything is fine." They'd even go out of their way to ensure their operational cables read as if they were written by men. A male COS advised one female case officer in Station in 1984 to edit out the first name of her pseudonym and any pronoun references that identified her as a woman.[4]

Only a handful of women had made it into DO management by this time, and this was particularly true for field management. Further, I was told, some of those who did, didn't want to be helpful to other women. One female officer, who was out of the office just three weeks to travel to a medical facility elsewhere in the country to give birth, learned when she returned to Station that her female manager had already started assigning her cases to other officers. The assumption was that once she had her baby, she would quit.

The few women in the DO who became operations officers were now focusing their efforts on securing sought-after recruitment cases—the types of cases that are instrumental in obtaining promotions. However, as I learned from interviews, the widely held belief among their male counterparts at that time was that women simply couldn't recruit assets, and so, they were often given operational handling cases—assets who were already recruited—or safehouse keeper responsibilities. The thought being that women had families and would not have the time necessary to develop a source to the point of recruitment. Never mind the fact that men had families, too, but that didn't seem to keep them from recruiting! Even so, women continued to prove their male detractors wrong, and the increase in female case officers meant women no longer felt like they were on an island as the lone woman in their stations. Lucy, for her part, spent much of the eighties "in grade" at headquarters, and she wasn't the only woman not getting promoted at this time. (The snail's pace of women's promotions would soon come to a head and in a very big way.) She did, however, secure her first role as deputy chief of station, although it wasn't as fulfilling as she had expected. Her COS wasn't exactly a champion of women, telling her after meetings, "I'd prefer you not talk too much."[5]

Janine was still experiencing success as she rose through the leadership ranks. And although it would be years before she'd realize it, she was actually rocketing straight toward a crash.

Janine

At the start of the eighties, Janine was a year into a successful tour in South America, where she served as acting deputy chief of station for some time. There was some occasional friction in Station, but overall, her chief was supportive of her work. She even managed to recruit a Soviet diplomat during her time there. As a result of her success in that post, Janine secured a follow-on assignment in New York.[6] By this time, her son, Steven, was away at college, and her and Colin's daughter, Tam, was at boarding school, so Janine lived alone in a nice two-bedroom apartment on Second Avenue.[7,8,9,10]

The streets of New York in the eighties were lined with women walking in their power suits with big shoulder pads and tennis shoes. The air was filled with optimism for women's rights. It was still considered significant for women to be in professional positions at the time, and as the head of her unit, Janine was well-liked by the officers who reported to her. She took her position as a role model seriously, even mentoring junior officers in the office, like Angela*.[11,12,13,14,15]

"I couldn't have been better off in terms of having women who are role models, women who had made it, despite men doing everything they could to keep you from joining the club," Angela told me of her time working for Janine in New York. As one of very few Black women in the DO, Angela was keenly aware that she always had to be twice as good and that some people were merely "tolerating" her presence. Having a manager like Janine meant that Angela had an advocate and mentor. While nurturing, Janine also held high standards for herself and for others. She took the mission seriously and bore the brunt of the harassment of male superiors so her reports wouldn't have to.[16]

"It wasn't easy for her, but she was very gracious and grateful," another female case officer who worked for Janine in New York told me.[17] Station officers never knew what might happen when they went into the office each day. They often worked unpredictable hours—staying late into the night. Janine thrived in that type of environment, and her hard work paid off in the types of targets she and the other officers were able to recruit.[18]

Despite the demanding hours, Janine made it a point to bring the staff together to get to know each other, so that they'd work better as a team. She invited officers to her home, and such gatherings didn't feel like work parties attended out of obligation. These were the type of get-togethers officers looked forward to and enjoyed. On the occasional Saturday, Janine went shopping with her friends from Station and elsewhere, listening to their personal dilemmas and providing sound advice. The friendships she formed in New York, just like every other Station in which she served, were friendships Janine maintained throughout the course of her life. She was nothing if not loyal.[19]

While in New York, Janine worked closely with the FBI, as did her ex-husband, Colin, who occasionally came into town. During this time, Janine and Colin began seeing each other again, a fresh start for what would become a lifelong companionship.[20]

Colin was working in counterintelligence alongside a colleague named Aldrich Ames. Colin handled Eastern European cases, and Ames, the Soviets. Ames volunteered to go to New York for a large event, and while there, he stayed in a safehouse with his Colombian girlfriend. This didn't sit well with Janine, and she shared her concerns with the chief that Ames was a security risk, running around using the safehouse as his own personal honeymoon cottage. But the COS ignored her. Eight years later, Ames would plead guilty to espionage on behalf of the Soviet Union that he began while Janine was serving in New York.[21,22]

Back at headquarters, there was still much work to do in the fight for gender equality, especially when it came to women of color. Carmen was asked to take the same multicultural course again. The exact same course. When she asked why, she was told that the course "didn't work unless there were people of color who were willing to speak up." Carmen wrote the head of analysis and said, "This is horrible for my career . . . to be in this room and people think I'm that person. I know these things need to be said, and I'm fine to say it authentically the first time, but not again and again."[23]

Angela, by this time, had finished her tour in New York and returned to headquarters, where she was preparing for a PCS assignment in sub-Saharan Africa. One day when she was walking through the headquarters cafeteria, a group of women case officers pulled her aside. They heard where she was heading. "Please don't go work for him," they pleaded. They explained that the outgoing COS was racist and sexist.

"In Africa Division, they always called people the N-word in the office," Angela told me, noting that hearing a COS was racist wasn't necessarily surprising to her. She went anyway. She wanted to make a difference. But working for him proved to be much worse than she expected.

"I was young and stupid," Angela said. She served almost two years when she was evacuated after becoming the target of a foreign intelligence service as a result of political events. Angela spent another year at the Agency, and in the end, she decided it was too much of a sacrifice to continue her career there. "When you have those experiences, you might have eighty-five percent great. But that fifteen percent is hurtful and demeaning and discouraging," she told me. Moreover, her personal life was limited. Angela longed for a life where she didn't have to worry about leaving dead drops or signaling. And so, in 1989, she left the Agency and didn't look back.[24]

In full transparency, one of the biggest challenges while writing this book was finding women of color who worked at the Agency. I can't help but wonder: How many women of color had experiences like Angela's, prompting them to leave the organization? And with the departure of these talented, competent women, how many intelligence successes were we robbed of?

Janine returned to Washington and bought a home in Georgetown where she continued to spend time with Colin, but they never lived together.[25,26,27,28] He kept his own home in Rockville, Maryland, and the two vacationed, raised dogs and cats together, and, simply put, enjoyed each other's company. In 1989, Janine was given her next assignment—COS in a Caribbean country. She had a good reputation, and the deputy director of the CIA for Operations (DDO) wanted to give her a COS position. And so, she was placed in Latin America Division, making her the first woman chief of station in Latin America.[29,30,31,32]

Unfortunately, this post was considered a CIA station from hell, the Agency's dumping ground with reports of wife-swapping and group gropes. Far from a tropical paradise one might imagine, like many countries in the Caribbean, it was incredibly dangerous. Station and embassy employees lived in compounds with armed guards and barred windows.

"If they come into your house, most likely they will kill you. They will rob you and rape you and then butcher you . . . your house is enclosed by iron grills. You have an alarm system and a safe-haven part of the house behind bars—nicknamed the rape gate," one former embassy employee said.[33]

Even so, Janine accepted the assignment and went alone. By this time, her son, Steven, was at Dartmouth, and her and Colin's daughter, Tam, lived with Janine's nephew. Colin visited Janine periodically, at least half a dozen times, staying anywhere from a week to two weeks each visit. He and Janine explored the island together, every nook and cranny they could find. Even the places where foreigners didn't usually venture.[34]

The dynamics in Station proved to be extremely difficult for Janine. For starters, finding people to serve there was difficult. There was little work there in terms of targets—mostly narcotics—which meant you didn't have your pick of the most solid officers, as top-tier talent and judgment could be put to greater use elsewhere. Colin was familiar with one particular officer who was in the running for a Station placement, whom he warned Janine about. That officer's father was a senior support officer, but she was unreliable, often not showing up for work.

"Don't take her," he told Janine.

But eventually, she did anyway. She didn't have much of a choice, since no one else would take the slot. And just as Colin predicted, the female officer rarely came into work, and if she showed up at all, she was often in her pajamas. Even worse, she was unreliable in her operations—not meeting or paying her assets—and told people she worked for the CIA if she had too much to drink.[35,36,37,38]

As if all of that wasn't enough of a security risk for Janine to worry about, she became aware that her deputy was physically abusing his wife to the point of hospitalization. When Janine reported the domestic violence back to headquarters, she didn't find a sympathetic ear.[39,40] That wasn't the only dangerous and uncomfortable information Janine reported back to Washington though. She also cited another officer who allegedly threatened to kill his local security guards.[41]

In spite of the difficulties, Janine, by all accounts, had a successful tour as COS. She formed a positive relationship with the ambassador, and when she returned to headquarters, she was preparing for a tour in Europe, a handsome reward after serving in a station from hell. That next tour, however, wouldn't come to fruition. Janine's career and life were about to take a very unexpected turn.

NAME: JACQUELINE*
YEAR OF BIRTH: 1948
PLACE OF BIRTH: PARIS, FRANCE
ENTRANCE ON DUTY: 1986
FIELD TRADECRAFT CERTIFICATION: YES
**HOME BASE: SPECIAL CADRE ON CHEMICAL BIOLOGICAL WARFARE
    TARGETS**
FOREIGN LANGUAGE: FRENCH

While Janine had multiple tours under her belt, Jacqueline*, a French American who immigrated to the United States later in life, was beginning a new chapter at the CIA, and by the end of the decade would be full steam ahead on running her own operations, both unilaterally and jointly with foreign liaison partners in a variety of aliases. Jacqueline acknowledges that the CIA was certainly still an old boys' club when she joined, and for many years after that, but that didn't stop her from having a fulfilling career.

"I was happy, performing, and didn't really care about anything else," she told me one day over Zoom from her home in Northern Virginia. The now seventy-six-year-old lights up when talking about her previous life in the shadows—a life she has chosen to keep private even now, years after her retirement. Jacqueline attributes much of her success to the fact that she was not only bilingual and well-educated, but also a psychologist. She could blend in with other cultures, and she understood how people reacted, what made them tick, and how to take authority, especially with men. She was told on more than one occasion by male operations officers that she was "a natural."

Perhaps one of the biggest contributing factors to Jacqueline's success, however, was that she joined the Agency in her late thirties in the 1980s, after having already lived the life of a stay-at-home mom and supportive wife. She kept herself busy during the early years of motherhood, volunteering at her children's school, socializing with other housewives at "lady lunches," and playing the role of devoted corporate wife, which often included international travel together with her husband. Once her children were school-aged and more self-sufficient, Jacqueline decided what she was doing no longer felt satisfying to her. It was time to go back to work.

Years earlier, Jacqueline had faced a crossroads. Would she get married and start a family or would she pursue a PhD in psychology? She chose the former. *I'll give myself up to my kids,* she decided. Now, she was starting to think perhaps it was time to revisit her desire to begin a doctoral program. But life threw her for a loop when she instead began a career at the CIA.

Jacqueline spent her first few years at the Agency providing linguistic support in various capacities, including clandestine operations, until one day a colleague told her she was "switching to the other side" and asked Jacqueline if she'd like to switch as well.

"I asked her, 'What is the other side?' I didn't even know!" Jacqueline laughingly said to me. But she soon found out. Her request to transition to the DO was granted, and she immediately went through an accelerated version of the Farm to receive her ops certification. She was assigned to a special cadre going after chemical and biological warfare (CBW) targets, which she told me was made up of an equal number of men and women. Over the next decade, she was involved in crucial, effective multitargeted operations.

"That's what really made me love that work and love the Agency," she told me.

Jacqueline says maturity and her wealth of life experience allowed her to be very effective at the operations she led—and there were many, all of them too secretive for her to go into detail. For example, she is the only woman to this day to have done one particular highly classified operation, about which she remains tight-lipped. She promises me that she'll tell me more about the fascinating work she's done over lunch one day, "just between you and me." I promise myself that I'll hold her to it.

Jacqueline's experience is similar in some ways to those of other women in the CIA in the eighties, but in other ways, it's strikingly different. I can't help but wonder if starting her Agency career after the early, more demanding years of motherhood allowed her the ability to escape some of the "will she/won't she" speculation over whether she would become pregnant, thus earning her more credibility from the get-go as a female operations officer. Or, perhaps, after having already lived through some of life's more "mundane experiences," as she called them, she was more appreciative of the exhilarating feel of espionage—so much that, as she said, she "didn't care about anything else."

An accomplished—and now retired—female operations officer, Jacqueline was happiest when she was away from the desk and in the field. She regularly ran joint operations with foreign partners, and in a moment she'll never forget, one of her liaison partners asked her, "How do you do it? Could you come tell our female officers how you succeed? Your targets don't see you as a woman."

"Because I'm a professional," she told them.

But it was more than her professional demeanor that made her so successful; along with a myriad of other factors, it was also Jacqueline's dedication to the mission. "The mission was number one, everything else had to follow. The mission was sacred. It cannot be sold to the highest bidder," she told me. She did not offer reflection on the implicit mutual understanding that it was a compliment not to be "seen as a woman."

It was that lock-hard focus on the mission that allowed her to thrive even when surrounded by men who believed women weren't capable of the job. That wasn't all men though, she told me. She remembers one chauvinistic deputy who, after working with her, came to believe that female operations officers had much better skills and were more successful [than men]. That deputy continued to champion female officers as he rose through the Agency ranks, which told Jacqueline that, despite the old boys' atmosphere, change was in the air.

As Jacqueline suspected, the eighties were proving to be both productive and pivotal for women in the DO and across the organization. Indeed, many female operations officers were beginning to recruit assets who produced high-level intelligence reports—proving that women could, in fact, recruit just as well as men, perhaps even better in some cases. One of the reasons for the change?

"Women started talking to each other," one senior CIA operations officer said in a classified discussion approved for release. It wasn't that they hadn't *wanted* to talk to each other. It was more like, they *couldn't*. Being an operations officer is by nature a lone-wolf occupation—it requires running surveillance detection routes throughout cities for hours at a time and one-on-one meetings with intelligence assets. But for female case officers, it could be even lonelier.

In the first few decades of the CIA, women case officers almost never encountered another woman in their field stations. They would return after their operational meetings—that is, if they were lucky enough to be allowed to run operations—to a station filled with men who may or may not be supportive of their work, and it was usually the latter.[42] There was no instantaneous connection like there would be years later over Sametime instant messenger and, later, Skype. The primary way of communicating from the field at the time was through cables, which didn't allow for women to keep in touch. You could email, once that became possible, but even that was a COS-by-COS decision. And in the DO, the COS was godlike. What he (because it was almost always a "he") says goes.

Moreover, there were plenty of women who maintained a "pay your dues" mentality—one I can attest still existed in some parts of the Agency two decades later—particularly in the DO. In spite of that, a small group of about twenty-five women formed the DO Women's Advisory Council (DOWAC) in the mid-eighties. Chaired by a GS-12 female case officer named Patty—because no one else would take the job [for fear of reprisal]—the DOWAC's mission was to advise the deputy director of the CIA for operations (DDO) on the hiring, training, and promotion of women.

When Patty became the chair, the council had already been in existence for three-plus years yet had never actually met with the DDO. She made it a priority to change that. Patty and another woman scheduled a meeting with DDO Dick Stolz to share their ideas with him. They had gotten the statistics from the career management staff, now called HRS, on the lack of women on DO promotion panels and highlighted the dismal numbers. In response, they received a four-page memo from DDO Stolz, which they initially viewed as not particularly encouraging and suspected was written by lawyers. Soon after, however, they were at least beginning to see women and minorities on promotion panels.[43]

At one point, DDO Stolz came down from the seventh floor to meet with the entire DOWAC to answer questions they had sent up to him. (The seventh floor is the location of the offices of the most senior CIA officials.) After going through each question, he had one for them. "Any of those of you who have experienced sexual harassment, would you please raise your hand?" To his credit, those present recall that he became furious when the hand of every single woman in the room went up. This marked the beginning of the Agency's zero-tolerance policy toward sexual harassment—though policy and actual implementation would prove to be two very separate issues, as we'll see in the years ahead.[44]

NAME: MARY BETH LONG
YEAR OF BIRTH: 1963
PLACE OF BIRTH: CENTRAL PENNSYLVANIA
ENTRANCE ON DUTY: 1986

FIELD TRADECRAFT CERTIFICATION: YES
HOME BASE: LATIN AMERICA
FOREIGN LANGUAGE: MANDARIN

While senior women were meeting in the eighties to ensure the continued success of women in the DO, Mary Beth was just starting out. One of three daughters, Mary Beth told me her parents always knew she was the one who would leave home one day.

"She marches to the beat of a different drum," her parents would say. They themselves were not college educated, but they knew Mary Beth was destined for not just higher education but also great things. She was a voracious reader, highly intelligent, and successful at school. She decided to attend Penn State, and while there, she learned Mandarin. She went to Taiwan as part of a semester exchange program and then was fortunate to have her honors counselor arrange for her to take time off and travel through China on her own in a personal capacity.

When she returned, just shortly before graduation in 1985, Mary Beth's professor told her there was a CIA recruiter in town and asked whether she wanted to meet with him. After having a taste of the overseas life, she knew she was mostly interested in living abroad. But when she met with the recruiter, he didn't allude to the DO at all. Instead, he talked about being an image analyst and a reports officer. And even then, he noted more than once that she was "too young."

Because Mary Beth had been abroad, her application took longer to process, and so she took a job with an Arab bank that allowed her to travel more—this time to Amman and Beirut, further cementing her desire to live overseas.

By 1986, Mary Beth reported for duty at Langley.

"Is there anyone who doesn't know what job you're here for?" one of the instructors at her orientation asked.

Six women raised their hands, including Mary Beth. She knew she was hired into the DO as a GS-8, but she wasn't sure what position. All six women wanted to be case officers, but they were told they were too young and they had to be reports officers instead. A few weeks passed, and Mary Beth, along with the other women, learned that there were plenty of men who were their same age who came in directly as case officers.

"You'll do reports for a few years," they'd tell her. "No Chinese will meet with you anyway because you're too young."

It sounded fishy and not like what she'd thought she'd signed up for. They wouldn't give her operational training. She and the other women were beginning to feel like this was a bait and switch. They wanted to be case officers, but each time they asked, they were dismissed.

"We'll think about it," the instructors would say. There were about sixty people in her Entrance on Duty (EOD) class, the cadre of officers who began their Agency careers on the same day, which included fewer than twenty women. Not one of whom was a case officer.

During one of Mary Beth's interims, an older CO gave her some honest, and crucial, advice. "You need to get off this track, because you'll be a second-class citizen. You'll always be the person who started as reports."

But the more Mary Beth insisted they make her a case officer, the more frustrated East Asia (EA) Division became with her. They decided they were done with her. They didn't want someone who didn't want to be a reports officer. She'd have to find a sponsor. While EA Division told her not to let the door hit her on the way out, Mary Beth was pleased when some senior male officers from Latin America Division went to bat for her. And they had good news—LA Division would sponsor her to go to the Farm for operational training.

In the time leading up to the Farm, Mary Beth went to an undisclosed field station, where she gave language lessons to long-term visiting Chinese citizens. She was incredibly productive, turning several intelligence targets over to Station, at which point EA made a play to get her back.

"Too late," LA Division told them. "She's ours."

While down at the Farm, Mary Beth and her classmates were called into the auditorium. A senior LA Division officer began by saying, "We've never done this before . . . ," and then proceeded to explain that he was there to give an Exceptional Performance Award to a trainee. Mary Beth was shocked and embarrassed to learn it was for her. More than anything, she felt awkward. As she walked down the hallway afterward to put her award in her safe, one of the instructors who was known to be a drunk, stopped her.

"Congrats. How'd you like working with Tom?" he said, giggling.

"Fine," she told him, unsure of why he was giggling. It wasn't until she graduated months later that she learned the reason.

"I gotta be honest with you," that same instructor said. "Several of us were wondering how many blow jobs it took. You have good skills, and people underestimate you." That was his way of apologizing.

On graduation day, during her outbriefing, a different instructor pulled her aside. "I gotta tell you when you were first assigned to me, I thought, *Oh, my God, they gave me the pixie.* No, no, don't be offended," he said after seeing her facial expression. "You have to give us guys from Vietnam a break. You're extremely attractive. You're very successful. Our expectations are frankly pretty low. You'll find later on, everyone is

going to underestimate you. Use it. Your journey will be to figure out how to be comfortable. Everyone will want to be near
you because they'll hope you're interested in them. You need
to figure out how to use that advantage." And his last piece of
advice: "Everyone is going to wonder who you're sleeping with,
so you better get married."

Mary Beth took all the advice on board, including the latter
part. She married a case officer named Bob, and they deployed
to a station in Latin America (LA) as one of its few tandem couples. (LA Division had adopted a willingness to support tan-
dems earlier than others did, perhaps colored by difficulties the
division faced in recruitment and retention due to conditions
on the ground.) The environment at their field station was vol-
atile. There was no water in the station and no air-conditioning
anywhere. At one point, terrorists fired a missile across the top
of the building, hitting the top of the windows where they met
the roof. Rather than explode, it skidded across the building,
taking out all the air-handling units and the commissary. The
office's one other woman, an economist, left, and Mary Beth was
left with men who couldn't be bothered to take the necessary
step of pouring water down the toilet after using it. Even so,
she loved it there. When families were sent home, Mary Beth
and Bob stayed. She even got incredibly lucky and recruited an
incoming minister. She worked the counterterrorism target and
thrived in her job even during this hardship tour.

As Mary Beth continued to find career success, however,
other parts of her life suffered. She and Bob were beginning to
feel that they had rushed things by marrying so quickly. (Even
years later, CIA officers often rushed into marriages in order to
make tandem assignments easier.) As her marriage crumbled,
she didn't have anyone to talk to; she had yet to meet a female
case officer other than her classmates back at the Farm. That's
when LA Division said they had a position opening as branch

chief back at headquarters. She accepted. Maybe it would give Bob some space to catch up with her success.

It wasn't enough. The two filed for divorce, and it was finalized after a year of being legally separated, as required in the state of Virginia. But it wasn't over between them. They dated for the next five years, but they never remarried. In fact, Mary Beth didn't ever remarry. When I asked if she felt that was a sacrifice, she said, "I consciously gave that up. It wasn't something that was all that important to me. I've loved my career. I don't regret it. I'll be honest with you. You cannot do it all. I don't know any woman who was a star case officer and also a mom. This balancing . . . don't fool yourself. Something's gotta give." And for Mary Beth, it was a marriage and family.

She found more and more success as a case officer, recruiting two or three assets on each tour. She played to her strengths. At one point, a manager suggested she wear a red dress, explaining, "You'll fall into a sea of badly dressed men, so wear your red dress. Insert yourself into the conversation. Hand out your cards."

She took his advice, and it turned out, he was right. When Mary Beth called potential targets from the party the next day and they had no idea who she was, she'd say, "I'm the woman in the red dress." It worked every single time. She'd ask if they were willing to go to lunch with her and capitalize on their being curious about what she wanted. She didn't care why they accepted the invitation; she just needed time on target. By the second meeting, she'd ask about their family. They'd realize she was smart, and over time, she'd change the relationship to one of colleagues and coconspirators.

Even with her success, Mary Beth still had skeptics. On one of her tours, she had six recruitments in the first year, two of them cabinet level. Soon after, she received a note from headquarters that said the branch chief was coming out to meet her asset. She pushed back—an emergency meeting like this with her asset made her uncomfortable. Instead, they arranged for her to take the asset to Washington, where she conducted a dinner with him and the branch chief. The next thing she knew, a counterintelligence team was coming out to do asset validation. Over the next several months and the remaining time in her tour, someone found a reason to meet with every single one of Mary Beth's important assets. At some point, she realized what they were doing. They didn't trust her. Years later, Mary Beth ran into one of the men who had conducted a fireside chat with her asset.

"Others were jealous," he said. "At first, we thought you were fabricating. One of the people you worked with in the past was doing that."

And so they decided to do a full-court press on everyone she recruited and handled.

"There were a lot of people who don't understand how you could be so different," he told her.

"I'm not that different. I'm [just] the only woman in these environments." When she reflected on this decades later in her conversation with me, she reiterated, "There's something about the way we're wired as women. . . . Every recruitment I ever had said yes because they believed I cared about them. And I did."[45]

It seemed Mary Beth had "cracked the code" and learned how to use her perceived weaknesses as a woman to her advantage.

Mary Beth left the CIA in 1999 and went on to find enormous success in the foreign policy arena. In 2007, she became the first woman confirmed by the US Senate as an assistant secretary of defense, making her the first female civilian four-star military equivalent in the history of the Pentagon.[46]

Even with all the progress in the eighties—albeit in some parts of the CIA more than others—it was far from a sisterhood. The

DOWAC, although the start of some important changes, carried with it a stigma.

"They were waiting for us to go down in front of the Bubble and burn our bras, I'm sure," Patty said.[47]

Some women were still hesitant to help others, even in the DI, which was considerably more progressive than other directorates by this time.

Carmen remembered an awkward conversation over one of her quarterly champagne dinners with her closest female friends in the DI at the time. The women were lamenting about all the new young women the Agency was hiring and how these women expected it to be easy.[48]

"They're not going to get any help from me. I had to make it the hard way. They're going to have to do the same," one woman said.

And the others, with the exception of Carmen, agreed.

"I remember thinking, *God, that's not right. That we should expect them to do the same things we did*," Carmen told me.[49] Thankfully, there were other women who shared her view.

One day soon after becoming a division chief, Debra (who had just returned from studying at Harvard, finally with the Agency's backing) was asked to present at a training class. She was caught off guard when someone asked, "What are you doing to help other women now that you're a division chief?"

Debra was embarrassed that she hadn't given it much thought. She hoped she had done a good job mentoring the women who worked for her—after all, her division was primarily made up of women. Then Debra had an aha moment. *What would happen if I invited all the female executives to get to know each other?* she wondered. There weren't many of them, and she didn't have a sense of this group of women and whether they'd even be interested in attending. She invited them anyway. She didn't think it was going to be an Agency-sanctioned activity, but at the same time, she didn't want to be accused of not doing her job, so she asked them to come to her office one evening after work.

Although the total number of women in leadership positions was small, Debra was shocked at the high proportion of them who came. The women were primarily from the DI, but there was one from DS&T and two or three from the DO.

Notably, one even came just to declare that she would not be in the group. "The power resides with men; I'm not going to do anything to jeopardize my position," the woman said. But after the women started talking promotions and assignments, she became convinced to join them.

Debra found it important to clarify to me that this wasn't a group of women meeting to gossip about their personal lives. "It wasn't like, 'Mothers, let's get together and talk about our kids,'" she told me. "We didn't have them. And even if we did, we didn't talk about them. We didn't talk about our personal lives at all." And besides, most of the women who had found success at these senior levels weren't married. (Only one of the women was married and had one child.) Many said they chose not to marry because the demands of the job were such that it just didn't happen for them.

After the success of the first meeting, Debra got buy-in from her manager, a very senior woman, and soon after, the women received permission to meet off-site. Debra began hosting the meetings in her home in the evenings, and more and more women joined. The program grew, partly out of frustration that they could make it to GS-15 but couldn't seem to progress beyond that. "All of the assignments were made in the men's room," Amy, who created the reports officer career track in the DO, told me.

The women formulated a mission statement and some objectives that focused on identifying and promoting opportunities for women in the Agency, and after some time and significant preparation, they made an appointment to see the then executive director of the CIA, known as the EXDIR, the director's chief operating officer. Together, the women had formulated a goal to get the Agency to hire a contractor to come in and look at barriers to women in the Agency, including their assignments, promotions, tandem couples, etc. They were especially interested in how women obtained assignments, as there didn't seem to be a competitive assignment process for them. They became aware of a "list" that they believed was consulted when there was a job opening—a practice they wanted to end. And so, the women banded together to have meetings with younger women, establish guidelines, hold open forums, and bring their concerns to Agency leadership, all with an eye of shattering the glass ceiling and paving the way for a new generation of women at the CIA.[50]

CHAPTER 4

THE PROMISING YET PROBLEMATIC NINETIES

It would be easy to look back at the nineties and associate it with a rise of "Girl Power" and gender equality. We began the decade with Kurt Cobain, but by 1996, we had the Spice Girls. And by the end of the decade, we had Britney, bitch. Beyond cultural feminism, women made significant strides politically and professionally—women had secured for the first time the positions of attorney general, secretary of state, president of an Ivy league institution, and CEO of a Fortune 100 company.[1]

The nineties seemed exceptionally promising for gender equality; women were marrying later, pursuing higher education, and joining the workforce, Allison Yarrow notes in her book *90s Bitch: Media, Culture, and the Failed Promise of Gender Equality*. But things weren't exactly what they seemed.

"The more women assumed power, the more power was taken from them through a noxious popular culture that celebrated outright hostility toward women and commercialized their sexuality and insecurity," Yarrow said.[2]

Indeed, sandwiched between these music icons and historic achievements for women, there were *other* notable events in the nineties that shaped our collective cultural experience as it relates to women, and they didn't exactly add up to a picture-perfect image of "Girl Power."

Perhaps one of the most pivotal events for our collective perception of women in the nineties was that of Bill Clinton's affair with Monica Lewinsky. At the time, the internet was just starting to take off and the concept of cyberbullying didn't yet exist. That didn't stop countless media outlets from vilifying Lewinsky, who had joined the White House as a young unpaid intern—and the public couldn't get enough. *New York Times* columnist Maureen Dowd called her "a little nutty and a little slutty."[3]

"This is all sort of part of the water at the time, where the woman is the evil seductress—and the poor, weak man had no power to resist her," says Jennifer Pozner, a media critic and the author of *Reality Bites Back: The Troubling Truth About Guilty Pleasure TV.*[4]

The James Bond franchise was no stranger to this type of feminine trope—its many portrayals of the female spy had some of those very traits. But the fall of the Berlin Wall in 1989 didn't just signify the end of the Cold War. It was the end of the female spy as we knew her, at least on-screen. Up until now, the Bond Girl was often a one-dimensional stereotype in a Cold War storyline steeped in sexual advances and innuendo. Instead of playing into the slut-shaming that was hidden in the underbelly of the nineties, the tide was beginning to turn for the Bond Girl. And much of that had to do with who was at the helm of the ship.

Barbara Broccoli, daughter of the legendary James Bond producer Albert "Cubby" Broccoli, became a full producer in 1995 in light of her father's declining health. While both Barbara and her brother Michael G. Wilson took over the rights from Cubby at that time—he died a year later, in 1996—it's no secret in Hollywood circles that it's been the ironfisted Barbara who's been calling the shots. She's had creative control over every decision, from strategic ones like the direction of the franchise to the more minute details like dialogue.

"She brought the character and the franchise into the modern era without compromising what's entertaining about a Bond movie and very discreetly did away with some of the less inclusive things that were OK back in the '70s," said Universal chair Donna Langley, a friend of Barbara's. [5] Indeed, with Barbara steering the ship, the Bond franchise began to see more balance and inclusivity.

Meanwhile at the CIA, the following decade would include key milestones in the fight for gender equality, including the CIA's Glass Ceiling study in 1991 that documented gender discrimination and later, a class action suit that brought expectations for change in both the organization and the next generation of female intelligence officers. At the recommendation of women in the Senior Intelligence Service (SIS)—the women's mentoring group Debra created—then-director William H. Webster approved a study to determine if career advancement barriers existed for women and minorities at the Agency, preventing them from advancing into middle- and upper-level positions, commonly referred to as a "glass ceiling." The study surveyed 927 employees, led focus groups with 432 employees, and held in-depth interviews with an undisclosed amount of SIS officers and the top eleven Agency executives, and found that yes, mindsets and biases contributed to discrimination and artificial barriers for both women and minorities. For example, although women made up 40 percent of the workforce, they held only 10 percent of the SIS positions, the senior-most level at the CIA.

Among many other stereotypes and discriminating practices the study identified, some SIS interviewees and focus group participants expressed concern that promoting women and minorities would lower the standards because they were "less qualified than their white male peers." White women also reported "having to walk a fine line between the cultural directives of 'speak out more frequently' and 'don't be pushy or confrontational.'" They were either too assertive or not assertive enough. They also made pains not to sound "too emotional"—the kiss of death for any woman's career. Moreover, the focus groups found that the perception that family responsibilities could interfere with women's commitment to work impacted their selection for certain assignments. And while some female operations officers were serving in high-threat environments in the nineties, it was still considered a rarity. There was a strong undercurrent of skepticism: "Are you sure you want to go there as a woman?" and "Is this really a place a woman is going to thrive?" In the coming years, women would prove that they could do just that—they could thrive, even in the most dangerous and demanding locations.

As for Lucy, her career was winding down. She finally made it to New York, and she even served as chief of station in an undisclosed field location. In between her overseas tours, she had a successful rotational assignment at the Office of Congressional Affairs, which she described as a "dog-eat-dog" environment. Even so, Lucy thrived. The chief told her, "You are exactly the kind of person needed in this job," words of affirmation she had been seeking her entire career. She was there when she received a call that a slot was available in a prestigious country in Europe. A colleague asked her, "What do you want on your tombstone? 'Diplomat in Europe' or 'Branch Chief in headquarters'?"[6]

And so Lucy went to Europe, where she had a grand time. Soon after returning stateside, she decided it was time to retire.

She began a new chapter as a real estate agent in New York, where she lives now, enjoying Broadway shows and regular visits to the Met.[7]

Similarly, Janine was preparing for a new chapter of her own.

Janine

On the heels of her successful tour as station chief in the Caribbean from 1988 to 1991, Janine was set to begin a tour as chief of station in Eastern Europe, no doubt a reward of sorts for her impactful work—despite the questionable conduct of her officers—in the Caribbean. That all changed when she learned she was the target of an internal investigation.

"Guess what happened," Janine said to Colin. "I was just told by the [inspector general] that I'm under investigation." She didn't know much of the details at first. She immediately contacted her COS from her tour in East Asia, George K., who had become a champion of her and her work. He was just as shocked as Janine and Colin. George's wife, an administrative judge in the district, advised Janine to get a lawyer. Among the allegations: Janine was a "sexual provocateur" who had "made sexual advances toward male coworkers," and she drank on the job. (The latter, I find particularly amusing, given the amount of booze I saw flow through headquarters and various field stations during my time at the CIA.) The irony of these allegations wasn't lost on Janine. In her nearly twenty-plus years at the Agency, *she* had been sexually harassed by around a dozen men, including three married chiefs of station. She didn't report any of those instances, because she believed it would be "career suicide."[8] (From my research and my own personal experience, I can tell you that this is a sentiment shared by countless other women at the Agency throughout the decades.) Janine denied the allegations against her, claiming the officers were retaliating for her disciplining them.

"It was one hell of a surprise," Colin told me. "I personally know two of the charges weren't true because I was there when they supposedly happened." He also told me that Janine drank only on rare occasions. "She didn't keep a bottle in her desk drawer or her safe." (Also of note, drinking was such an ingrained part of CIA culture that there were regular happy hours at headquarters, and I knew plenty of officers who *did* keep booze in their desk.) One of the incidents in question was a farewell party for Janine that she arranged so case officers could meet some of her contacts. She worked in the office that morning, went out to lunch with Colin, and changed clothes at home before driving to the party. While walking in, she caught her heel on the grass where it joined the sidewalk and tripped a little, losing her balance for a second. That brief misstep turned into a charge that she was drunk at the party. (Full disclosure: This retelling is from Colin's perspective, who obviously brings his own bias to the table. That said, I'm having a difficult time understanding what the problem would be if in fact Janine *had* been drinking at her own farewell party. She certainly wouldn't have been the first COS to do that, nor would she be the last. And I think you'd be hard-pressed to find any male COS reprimanded for the same behavior.)

Janine was also accused of harassing an agent from the Drug Enforcement Agency (DEA) at that same party, where she allegedly "draped" herself across the man and "massaged his chest," telling him what she intended to do to him sexually. Seemingly grasping at straws, in addition to alleging that Janine had "imperceptible underwear," the report also alleged she claimed overtime for a Thanksgiving turkey dinner in which she hosted Station's local contacts in 1989 and misuse of Station's helicopter for picnics.[9]

Janine's legal team initially advised her to sign something and take the slap on the wrist, which would amount to losing her tour in Eastern Europe. The mindset was that as long as she 'fessed up, everything would be forgotten. They'd put a letter in her file. But that's not what Janine wanted. After all, she didn't have anything to "'fess up." She decided the best course of action—indeed, the *only* course of action—was to sue the Agency for sexual discrimination.

"I'm gonna fight it," Janine told her lawyer, Victoria Toensing. Certainly, by doing that, she knew it was the end of her career, regardless of the outcome. Janine continued working at headquarters throughout the investigation, but she lost access to just about everything and was seated at a typing credenza at the end of a hallway with nothing to do. Because she didn't do well sitting idly by, Janine began attending law school at George Washington University in the evenings.

The government's case against Janine, however, was on the verge of collapsing. As it turned out, the inspector general's (IG) interviews were incredibly one-sided. Margery, a close friend of Janine's, proactively reached out to the IG, Frederick Hitz, to speak on her behalf.

"I told him Janine was a fabulous manager and had solid tradecraft," she told me. But the IG didn't take any notes during the meeting. What's more, the Agency didn't interview the alleged victim from DEA. Janine knew if she could find the agent, he could vouch for her and explain that she did not sexually harass him. She went to the acting chief of DEA, Terry Burke, who had been in East Asia when Janine arrived. Terry was young, personable, and likable—not a hotshot. When Janine went to Terry and said she needed to find this DEA agent to corroborate her story, he leaped into action.

"As long as you don't besmirch the name of the DEA or cause any harm, I'll help you," he told her. She agreed, and he delivered. In an affidavit, the DEA agent refuted the accusation and said that Janine's "behavior had been impeccable and that no one at the inspector general's office had contacted him during its investigation."[10] He confirmed that she did not "massage my chest . . . touch me in any way that was sexually provocative . . . 'drape' herself on me . . . say anything that was sexually provocative."[11]

The CIA eventually settled, agreeing to pay Janine $410,000 plus $70,000 in legal fees in 1994, just three years after the Glass Ceiling study. The organization stopped short of admitting any wrongdoing, which her lawyer said was difficult for Janine.

"She wanted an apology," Toensing said.[12] When Janine graduated from George Washington University four years later, she and Colin celebrated with their friends by drinking champagne and eating crab cakes on a boat on the Potomac. Soon after, she passed the bar and began handling cases involving sex discrimination and whistleblowers at the CIA and other US government agencies. *The Washington Post* called her "a one-woman crusade to expose abuses taking place behind government walls."[13]

However, there were some women, who, even to this day, don't share that view of Janine. Though many of the people I interviewed about Janine described her as exceptional, there were a handful who had fewer positive things to say. One female case officer described Janine as "someone not to emulate," while another declined to comment on her, as she was a "controversial figure" at the time. One former case officer commented on her style of dress, which she said included sheer blouses and visible bra straps, noting she thought it "unprofessional."

"[Janine] was the first to gripe about being discriminated against. I looked at her thinking, *If you were walking around looking [like that]*," the woman told me. I bit my tongue and considered how often the slut-shaming of women comes from other women.

And then, in a real-life game of telephone, she told me, "She got four million dollars." Somehow, Janine's awarded sum of $400,000 had turned into a whopping $4 million. But the next thing she said was crucial. "I never worked with her directly." Indeed, all the negative comments about Janine I discovered in my research came from people who had never actually worked with her.

It's no surprise that the Agency can be a real gossip machine. We even had a name for it when I was there: RUMINT, which stood for rumor intelligence. You learned very early on to be mindful of what was added to your "hall file." And the DO in particular could be vicious. Personal sabotage through false sexual narratives occurred with surprising frequency, often targeting officers who had good jobs or were in line for good jobs, much like Janine. I found that the most reliable sources of information about Janine, who unfortunately passed away months before I began my research, were countless interviews with a range of individuals who worked with her over several decades, during her CIA career and long after, as well as personal friends and family. They revealed a woman who was one hell of a case officer and a true trailblazer for women like me who came long after. And even after everything she went through, she wasn't bitter.

"I feel free," Janine told a friend. "I feel focused on a new mission—helping other women. Although I wouldn't have asked for it to happen, it's made my life better."[14]

In 1995, a year after Janine's case, an undisclosed number of female operations officers received the validation they had been seeking when the CIA agreed to pay more than $1 million in back pay and salary increases to settle charges of gender discrimination. Joseph M. Sellers, the lawyer who represented the female operations officers in the class action suit, said it "should end an old-boy network whose demise is long overdue."[15]

I met Margery, the woman behind the class action suit, at her home in Northern Virginia on a humid summer day in June 2023. Dressed in lime green and blue with equally bright, matching eye makeup, Margery welcomed me into her home, where we sat on her screened-in porch and discussed what it was like being a woman in those early years at the Agency and what led her to file the suit.

Prior to our meeting, Margery had been described to me as eccentric, extravagant, and "a character." I found all of those descriptions to be accurate. There are so many other adjectives I'd add to the list though, like fearless, badass, funny, intelligent, resilient . . . a fucking legend. It should come as no surprise that she and Janine became close friends after serving at the same field station. (Of note, even Margery kept her distance from Janine at first because other officers had "poisoned the well." She had to learn for herself that Janine was an exceptional case officer and manager—and someone whom she would come to call a dear friend.) Margery was hired at a time when the Agency was trying to make it right—well, they were being forced to by federal law, to be exact—by hiring more women, but as she experienced on that first day of training, not everyone agreed that the women were qualified to be there.

Margery was used to dealing with discrimination from the beginning of her Agency career, but when it began to affect her promotions, that's when it really got under her skin. After twelve years in the DO, she had only been promoted twice, whereas most men had been promoted four times in a similar timeframe. What's more, she noticed a pattern from her very first performance appraisal review (PAR). At the beginning of her tour, Margery's COS put restrictions on her recruiting, encouraging her to "get her bearings" first. You can imagine how surprised she was when she read her PAR and saw she was dinged for not recruiting. She successfully challenged the review, and when it went to adjudication, the chief/Africa Division agreed that there was no justification as to why the COS limited her. The hold on Margery's recruiting was lifted, and in the next month, she made multiple recruitments. She had other successful tours after that, including more recruitments.

Having married a senior DO officer with kids of his own, Margery attributes her career success to her live-in help, a woman named Rosa. "She [Rosa] got me through my first twelve years [at the Agency]. I wouldn't have made it if I didn't have a 'wife,'" she says in her cheeky, yet completely serious way. That was also thanks to her mother, who advised her to "never try to do it all, because you will fail. Get a wife."[16]

When Margery filed the suit in 1992, as you can imagine, it was a long time coming. She was serving at a field station in Europe at the time, alongside Carmen, who distinctly remembers the day Margery filed the suit.

"She comes into my little office—'Carmen, guess what. I just filed my class action suit against the DO.' I was like, 'Oh my God, should I even be talking to you?'" Carmen believed Margery was doing the right thing, but she worried she'd get in trouble if people thought she was a friend of hers. "But I got over that," she told me. And it was a good thing, because if it weren't for Carmen, Margery felt utterly alone.[17]

When Margery returned to headquarters, she began actively marketing in the cafeteria, doing everything she could to rally women to join her. Now that she had filed, there was nothing the Agency could do to her. She felt invincible. I try to imagine my many days walking through the headquarters cafeteria and what it would have been like to have a woman standing at a table encouraging other women to sue the Agency for discrimination. It's almost unthinkable. Unimaginable. But it happened. And so much of me wishes I was there to see it. I'm in awe as I listen to Margery describe the atmosphere, and I lift up a silent prayer of thanks to the universe that she and I are able to meet and that I can experience these bits of history through her eyes.

Despite Margery's outspoken efforts, many women were afraid to rock the boat. Consider how many women had experienced this discrimination for decades, and yet the culture was such that women were afraid to speak up. They believed, as did Janine, that it would be career suicide. One woman told me that many of the women didn't want to be a part of a sisterhood or the "rebellion" they saw taking root.

"We wanted to opt out of the lawsuit," she told me. "We didn't want the money. We tried to give it back, but legally, we couldn't." She told me that a number of women used the money to buy a piece of jewelry to wear around the halls. She herself bought a bracelet and referred to it as her "women's money bracelet." She and others donated the rest of the money to charity.[18] Margery, however, told me a different story. She said there *was* a way to opt out and that they tracked those who refused the money. Not a single person.[19]

Megan, a female operations officer and legacy employee, recalled the atmosphere leading up to the class action suit when she entered on duty in 1993.[20] "I was approached multiple times by women in the organization that were looking for people to sign onto the class action suit."

Megan, however, was reluctant to add her name to the suit because she was brand-new to the Agency, and although she didn't discount the experiences of the women, it didn't reflect *her* experience thus far. What she'd come to realize later only with the benefit of hindsight, which she notes with a tinge of embarrassment, is that she wanted everyone to look at her as an operations officer and not a *female* operations officer. As one of only four women in her Farm class, she very much wanted to be treated like everyone else, and more than anything, she wanted to prove that she could be an operations officer, almost in *spite* of being a woman.[21]

Moreover, some officers were hesitant to join the suit due to the RUMINT around the building. Similar to some of the comments people made about Janine during my interviews, some officers spoke negatively about the women behind the class action suit. Lucy, for example, told me she was advised by a man not to get involved with "those people."

"The person doing this—she's not a good officer," he told her. "And the women who are trying to get promoted are not that good."[22] I couldn't help but wonder if this was a tactic to keep the women divided. To keep any semblance of a sisterhood at bay. When I spoke to Carmen, she gave me some important context that's worth highlighting.

"It's kind of irrelevant whether you're a good employee. It depends on the idea. It does help your idea if you're highly respected or there's no controversy surrounding you," Carmen told me. She went on to tell me that she's known Margery for thirty years, and while she can see what some of her "less strong areas" are, the reality is that if you're not a member of the ruling class, and in this case, she tells me that is white men, "your faults get magnified in ways that other people's don't get magnified."

Despite some of the naysayers, the class action suit was successful for the women who filed, and along with that success came a set of unrealistic expectations from the women who came before her, Megan told me. "They sort of turned to my generation of young women and said, 'Okay, now you can have it all.' Because they had never been given the latitude and the opportunity that we were given in the organization. The problem is that class action suit may have changed the window dressing for women . . . but it didn't change the fact that you're still the primary caretaker at home. You're still the primary with elder care issues, etc."

Like Megan, other female operations officers like Mary and Kathleen would soon learn that it would take much more than a million-dollar settlement to change an organization's culture. That certainly didn't stop them from trying.

NAME: MARY*
YEAR OF BIRTH: 1971
PLACE OF BIRTH: BEIRUT, LEBANON
ENTRANCE ON DUTY: 1994
FIELD TRADECRAFT CERTIFICATION: YES
HOME BASE: NEAR EAST DIVISION
FOREIGN LANGUAGES: FRENCH, ARABIC

If you ask Mary what she thinks about the Bond Girl, she'll tell you she's not a spy. When Mary joined the CIA in 1994, *GoldenEye* had yet to be released, and the image of the Bond Girl still conjured up less-than-favorable stereotypes—the kind Mary would soon learn she had to work against to be successful in her new job as a CIA intelligence officer.

Mary didn't intend to join the CIA. Like so many women who came before her, Mary had other plans. She wanted to become a lawyer. Sure, she had interned at the CIA over the summer while she was in college, but that was commonplace when you grew up in Vienna, Virginia, just down the road from Langley. It wasn't until a conversation with her father shortly after her graduation from the University of Virginia in 1993 that her plans for the future began to come into focus.

"What's the best thing you've done in your life?" her father asked, pausing for a brief moment before continuing. "You became a US citizen."

Mary knew where he was going next.

"And what do you think is the most valuable thing you can offer your country right now?" he asked his daughter before answering his own question again. "Your Arabic. It's a hard language to learn; you already have it. Think about joining the CIA to give back."

Having served as a captain in the Lebanese Army, Mary's father was no stranger to service, and he instilled this value in Mary, his eldest daughter, from a young age. Mary was born in Beirut in 1971, just four years before the onset of the Lebanese Civil War. And in the summer of 1975, Mary's family was spending time in the mountains when they returned to Beirut one evening to find a roadblock on their street.

"You can't pass. There's been a bomb," one of the guards told Mary's mother.

"I need to talk to my husband. He's a captain," her mother said as she pushed through to the guards manning the blockade. Mary's father had been splitting his time between their two apartments, spending weekends with the family in the mountains when he could and returning to Beirut for work. On this particular night, Mary and her sister were alone with their mother. Thankfully, the officers let her use their radio to contact him.

"You need to take the girls back to the mountains. It's not safe in the city," Mary's father told her.

The next time Mary and her family returned to their two-bedroom apartment that sat across the street from a Greek Melchite church, they stayed only one night—just long enough to pack their bags.

"My God, the smell. Did you smell that last night?" her mother asked her father the next morning.

"Yes, it's the smell of garbage and tires burning," he told her.

He put Mary, her mother, and her younger sister on a plane to the United States. They arrived in New England, where Mary's uncle had already immigrated. A doctor, he was now a

US citizen, married to an American woman with whom he had three sons. Over the next two years, Mary's father traveled back and forth from Lebanon to the United States, committed to fulfilling his military service, until one day he stopped.

"When are we going back?" Mary's mother asked him.

"We're not going back," he said.

"Okay, when are *you* going back?"

"I'm not."

An argument about what to do with furnishings and cars ensued, but it became clear there would be no more traveling back and forth for any of them. They would stay in the United States. After two years in New England, Mary's father secured a job with a defense contractor, prompting the family to establish roots in Vienna, Virginia. Her parents considered themselves Western leaning—they met while studying in Europe on scholarship in the late sixties—even giving Mary and her sister Western names, so immigrating to the United States didn't come out of left field. In fact, if it weren't for her father's desire to fulfill his military service, he and Mary's mom would have left Lebanon years ago. Mary knew how lucky she was to have escaped a childhood in Lebanon while the country was engulfed in a civil war that in the end claimed an estimated 120,000 lives[23]— she thanked God every day her parents made the decision to leave. But more than that, she couldn't imagine growing up in Lebanese society with all the demands on women to look and behave a certain way, which were completely inconsistent with her values.

And so, Mary grew up in a three-story white colonial on a quiet suburban street in Northern Virginia, thousands of miles away from the bombings in Beirut. She was a self-proclaimed "tomboy," who learned early that she was just as capable of achieving what she wanted as the boys were. It was also important to Mary's father that she and her sister know how to defend themselves, so he enrolled them in karate—tae kwon do Korean-style, which they did for about three years. (She would later use these skills to defend herself from bullies in elementary and middle school.) That's not to say that Mary didn't do other activities that were more stereotypically for girls. She took classical ballet classes from a Russian teacher, frequently performing with the advanced classes during recitals. But her true love was soccer. She was athletic and driven, competing in tournaments all the way up to Canada and even as far as the United Kingdom.

This departure from strict stereotypical gender norms in Mary's home growing up meant that years later, when she joined the CIA in 1994, she was completely unaware of the set of unspoken rules for women there: Women shouldn't be operations officers, and if they were, they absolutely could not be married. If they somehow squeaked past these rules *and* decided to have kids, they could consider their careers over, especially if they wanted to go part-time. And when it came to women handling weapons or going into war zones? That posed even more challenges.

But Mary didn't know these rules, so when her interviewer for Near East (NE) Division asked her, "Won't it be hard to be a female operations officer and work in the Near East?" she answered matter-of-factly: "Well, to be honest, men will want to speak to me before they'll want to speak to you."

It was that confidence, and perhaps a little naivete, that allowed Mary to hit the ground running at the CIA. To be fair, plenty of CIA officers, especially new ones coming through the door, didn't know these implicit rules. After all, it was the nineties, and it seemed women were gaining more—not less—ground when it came to gender equality, at least on the surface. (Let's not forget about all the socially acceptable slut-shaming that happened during this decade that we've only now, decades later, begun to recognize and truly understand.) The culture among women was still more competitive than helpful, and women often had to learn these rules the hard way.

Before going to the Farm for several months of demanding operational training, Mary worked three interims to get to know headquarters and the business of intelligence—a requirement for all Clandestine Service Trainees (CSTs). Her first interim was as a desk officer on an ops desk, mostly running name traces and supporting operations in the field; the second as a collections management officer (CMO), the new official name for a "reports officer," the go-between for the operations officers in the field and the analysts at headquarters; and a final interim in a non-DO role in the DS&T. During her CMO interim, while working for a woman named Gina Haspel, who would go on to become the CIA's first female director in 2018, Mary attended a meet and greet with NE Division operations officers.

"I'd like to go to NE Division after the Farm," Mary told a senior NE ops officer. "I speak Arabic and French, and I spent my early childhood in Lebanon, so I think I'm a good cultural fit."

"Let me get this straight: you're a woman, you want to be an ops officer, *and* you want to go to NE Division? Could you possibly make life any harder for yourself?"

But Mary wasn't daunted. Months later, she traveled to the Farm to obtain her field tradecraft certification, which would officially make her an operations officer. It was common for some CIA officers to "wash out" of the Farm, returning to headquarters without the esteemed ops certification, but instead, a permanent stain on what CIA officers call their "hall file." The officers would be assigned to some other position at headquarters, not nearly as exciting as what they hoped they would do as an operations officer in the field.

"*Ma tiswadi wuj al-ayleh*," Mary's Lebanese mother said to her before she departed for her grueling months at the Farm, which Mary told me roughly translated to "You will not blacken the face of this family." She was essentially telling Mary, "If you go to this training, you *will* finish." Although she was a stay-at-home mom for much of Mary's childhood, she was an extremely educated woman, having had a career before motherhood and subsequent ones after her children were grown. She was a woman who believed in setting goals and achieving them.

Life at the Farm, as it turned out, came naturally to Mary. Having grown up in a Lebanese household where her family hosted frequent dinner parties in their home, Mary knew how to talk to people, especially her elders. It seemed this was the perfect preparation for the role-playing she would do with her Farm instructors, who were generally senior or retired operations officers who had spent decades in the field. They used that experience to teach new operations officers everything they needed to know through countless role-playing exercises, in which they pretended to be the assets. But just because it came naturally to her didn't mean Mary coasted. She spent a lot of time working and often stayed on the weekends when others went home so that she could finish her work.

Of all the conversations Mary had while at the Farm, it was the advice she received from one of her female instructors that would stay with her for the entirety of her career and long after.

"Never cry in front of your male manager. He won't know how to handle it, and it's not fair to him," she told Mary.

"It started right then, me learning that I had to fit into a man's world. Not a shared world where I could be myself, but a world defined by men for men, and where to be successful, I needed to behave like a man as well," she told me decades later.

It wasn't just that piece of advice that stuck in Mary's mind about her time at the Farm though; there was another conversation that would haunt her and serve as a reminder to trust her gut. After a surveillance detection exercise one day, Mary sat across from her instructor at a café to receive feedback on how she did on the run. It was common for students to meet their instructors in such settings to role-play an ops meeting or to receive feedback from the exercises. The two talked back and forth over coffee as he reviewed Mary's route, and at one point, Mary laughingly retold what her father had always told her to look for if she was trying to catch a spy. *Follow the money*, he told her. The conversation moved on, but her instructor, a man named Jim Nicholson, circled back.

"Now what else did your dad say to look for if you were trying to catch a spy?" he asked her. Mary's hands began to shake.

What the hell is wrong with me? she thought to herself. She carefully moved her hands to her lap, hiding them under the table so her instructor wouldn't see them trembling. *Oh my God. I'm sitting in front of the next Aldrich Ames*, she thought.

Ames had been arrested just one year earlier for spying for nearly ten years for Russia. The Agency was still trying to repair the damage he had done. And yet, in this moment, something about Nicholson's words and demeanor convinced Mary that he was following in Ames's footsteps. But who could she tell? Who would believe a junior CIA officer who hadn't even graduated from the Farm? And if they didn't believe her, she could kiss her hopes of receiving her ops certification goodbye. Best to stay quiet and not rock the boat, she decided. She was probably just overreacting anyway, right?

Months later, in December 1995, Mary returned to headquarters having earned both her ops certification, graduating in the top three of her class, and securing a spot in NE Division. The following spring, she learned she had an opportunity for an extended TDY to a location in the Near East to fill in an under-lap in Station for several months.

A few days before she departed, her colleague Tony finally worked up the nerve to ask her out.

"We'll talk about it when I get back," she told him. *Why start something up right before leaving town?* she thought to herself.

"At least grab some lunch with me in the cafeteria," he insisted, and she agreed.

Tony brought his best friend, Alex, along to the lunch. Alex was an analyst in the DI, but he was already in the process of what was called "gatewaying" into the DO to become an operations officer. Mary wasn't so much thinking about dating prospects at the lunch; her thoughts were focused on her upcoming TDY. She hadn't considered dating Tony before he asked her out, and as for Alex—well, he was nice enough, but Mary had preconceived notions about unreliable womanizers. That changed a few months later, when Mary was still overseas, and Tony reached out to invite her to Alex's family's vacation home in Europe for some R&R. She had been working hard, and a European getaway sounded enticing, and so she thought, *Why not?*

Within a couple of days at Alex's place, she knew *he* was the one she was interested in—not Tony. And so, true to form, Mary was straightforward and direct with Tony.

"You're already breaking up with me?" he asked her.

"We'd have to have been dating first to break up!" she told him. While a little awkward at first, there was no denying the spark between her and Alex. More than that, she felt comfortable around him and appreciated his warm, welcoming personality. Far from an unreliable womanizer, he was a genuinely good guy. A few nights into the trip, she and some others were out at a local bar when two men started hitting on her. Alex spotted the interaction from afar and sensed how uncomfortable Mary was. It was then that he swooped in, unsolicited, and said, "Hey! There you are!" putting his arm around her, smoothly extricating her from the situation. It wouldn't be the last dicey situation the two of them would get out of together.

Mary and Alex decided to continue their relationship despite the distance between them while Mary finished up her extended TDY. She returned to the States months later, and Alex picked her up from the airport. He had essentially moved into her apartment when she was gone, and the two remained inseparable moving forward.

On one of the rare occasions when they were apart after her return to the States, Alex called with some news.

"How's the trip?" she asked him enthusiastically.

"Well, I'm not exactly on TDY. Listen, I want you to turn on your TV when we get off the phone. I'm not in trouble, and you're not in trouble," he said measuredly. "But once you turn on the TV, you'll understand why I'm not where I was supposed to be this week."

Mary hung up the phone and reached across the table for her remote to switch on the television.

"Holy shit," she said.

As far as Mary knew, Alex departed a few days earlier for a TDY with his branch chief and another CIA officer. What she didn't know, however, was that Alex never made it off the runway at Dulles International Airport that night. As he and his colleague were awaiting the arrival of their branch chief on the plane preparing for departure, an announcement over the PA system called for the two of them to leave the aircraft. At the bottom of the steps, Alex was greeted by the chief of NE Division, who informed the two of them that they would be taken to a nearby hotel for the next few days until things blew over. As Alex looked over on the tarmac, he saw his branch chief, Jim Nicholson, being handcuffed and put into a squad car.

Jim Nicholson. Mary's surveillance instructor from the Farm.

She felt a pit in her stomach as she watched the news coverage. She'd been right about him. Nicholson was arrested on November 16, 1996, for spying on behalf of Russia. In a joint CIA-FBI press release, Director of Central Intelligence John Deutch said, "The arrest of Nicholson is the direct result of an unprecedented level of cooperation between the CIA and the FBI. We are now able to demonstrate quite conclusively that the post-Ames reforms work as designed. Clearly the post-Ames analysis and detection mechanisms the CIA and FBI put in place succeeded in the identification of Nicholson and his alleged espionage activities on behalf of the Russian intelligence service."[24]

The interrogations of CIA officers came swiftly after the arrest. Nicholson was widely believed to have had several affairs with his female students at the Farm, but no one knew which ones, which meant Mary was summoned for questioning by the FBI and the CIA's Counterintelligence Center (CIC). She was interrogated for hours—first by FBI agents and then by CIC officers. They watched from behind the glass and then asked her the same questions. They had to ask directly due to chain of custody; they also used it as an opportunity to look for inconsistencies in her story.

"You lied to us! We know you had an affair with Nicholson," one of the FBI agents accused her.

"You guys were watching him. I want you to point out any indication where I told you that I wasn't with him but I was. If you don't believe me, put me on the box, but I'm not answering this question again," Mary said firmly. She'd had enough.

"How do you think you'd do if we put you on the box?" he asked smugly, referring to an Agency polygraph examination.

"I think I would pass because I know I'm telling the truth," she answered.

Mary left that day so angry she thought she'd resign. She reached out to a senior CIA officer she had known for years, prior to her career at the Agency. It seemed he had some pull over the investigation, because the next day when she went in for questioning, the FBI had a different tone. They offered their version of an apology, and the female FBI agent with whom Mary had shared her café story and early suspicions about Nicholson said to her, "Will you listen to your gut next time?"

"I will," Mary promised.

It was her first moment of female empowerment in her career. A reminder not to make herself small. To speak up when she knew something was wrong. When she knew it in her gut.

Mary and Alex became engaged a month later, in December, and married the following year just before Mary's first tour in the Near East. Alex accompanied as her spouse on her PCS orders—they were officially a "tandem couple"—and began Arabic training. Soon after, he went to the Farm to receive his ops certification, solidifying his transition to the DO as an ops-certified case officer.

Mary, on the other hand, was already putting her ops certification to work. Her first "real" operational meeting while PCS to the field was with an asset who had recently been recruited. So recent, in fact, that Mary's meeting with him was the first one after recruitment, notoriously the most difficult meeting you can have with an asset. She was more curious than nervous—a testament to CIA's exceptional training—but more than anything, she was annoyed. Station had sent another officer with her to drive the car, but she believed he was along to assess her abilities and report back to Station management. It was particularly annoying because Mary believed *she* was in fact the better officer, but it seemed not everyone in her management chain believed women could be successful operations officers. The meeting went off without a hitch, and she took over the case, which went on to be productive.

Mary was skilled enough to have not just one recruitment on her first tour but two. Some officers walked away from their first, and even subsequent tours, without any recruitments. It was dependent upon so many factors. (CIA officers and instructors, especially, love to tell you that "it depends" about virtually everything. And when it comes to the number of recruitments an officer can get on a tour, that statement certainly rings true.) But thankfully, for Mary, she got two under her belt.

Her second recruitment was a target she developed from the very first bump at a reception. From there she held a couple of one-on-one meetings with him and assessed his motivations and vulnerabilities. Assets can be motivated to work with the CIA for a whole host of reasons, and while for some people it was money, more often than not, Mary found that ideological reasons served as the most powerful driver. That was the case with this asset. He genuinely believed that the instability his country was facing could be improved if the United States were receiving more accurate intelligence that could inform its foreign policy. He was concerned for his country and felt that his cooperation with the Agency wasn't treason; it was the very opposite of that. It was his patriotic duty. The relationship was fruitful with only a few hiccups—the first being when he tried to hold Mary's hand.

"This is a business relationship," she told him point-blank. "It doesn't go any further than that."

Truth be told, she was disgusted. She wanted to break off the relationship right then and there, but she knew she couldn't. He was producing valuable intelligence, so she'd need to find a way to ensure the boundaries were clear. Soon after, Mary brought their spouses into the mix for social outings. That's when the next hiccup happened.

The asset's wife turned to her as she was walking out the door and said, "Mary, I know you're interested in my husband, and I want you to know I'd never do that to you," she said, looking Mary dead in the eyes.

Mary looked at her just as intently and said, "And I want *you* to know that I would never do that to you. This is a business relationship."

It was Mary's resilience and professionalism that allowed that case to continue to flourish, producing actionable intelligence. In addition, she hit all the important milestones on that first tour—from recruitments to number of intelligence reports to successful handling of her cases. Despite that, she was passed up for promotion, which Mary attributed in large part to her first COS not so much as mentioning her name back at headquarters. She couldn't help but think it had something to do with her being the only female operations officer in Station. *Wouldn't that be even more of a reason for her name to come up?* she considered. It was the second COS—who had a much more favorable (and accurate) view of female case officers and their capabilities—who successfully argued for Mary's promotion before the completion of her tour.

As the nineties came to a close, Mary was gearing up for her next assignment, feeling confident in her ability to do the job and ready to see where her second field tour would take her.

NAME: KATHLEEN*
YEAR OF BIRTH: 1970
PLACE OF BIRTH: SEOUL, SOUTH KOREA
ENTRANCE ON DUTY: 1996
FIELD TRADECRAFT CERTIFICATION: YES
HOME BASE: EAST ASIA DIVISION
FOREIGN LANGUAGE: KOREAN

At the same time Mary was beginning her first field tour, another new operations officer was learning the ropes at Langley: a first-generation Korean American named Kathleen. Like Mary, Kathleen spent her early childhood outside of the United States in a home that didn't adhere to traditional gender roles and societal expectations. In fact, it was her progressive-minded uncle, Yonghwa, who encouraged Kathleen to learn English early and prioritize her education while growing up in Seoul. Yonghwa was not so much into marriage as an institution but finally gave in sometime in his forties—particularly late for Korean culture. If he hadn't been the firstborn, he likely wouldn't have married at all. However, Yonghwa was keenly aware of his culture's expectations that he marry and have a son.

In the time before starting his own family, Yonghwa devoted much of his energy into influencing Kathleen. More than anything, he instilled his open-minded worldview, never qualifying her as a woman and instead, telling her she could do whatever she wanted, go wherever she wanted, and that education was the most important thing in achieving her goals and having a fulfilling life. This was a significant departure from the messaging most young women Kathleen's age were receiving in traditional Korean homes in the eighties—the expectation being that they go to college, meet a "good man" (meaning from a wealthy family), marry, have kids, and become a housewife.

But Kathleen's world opened up to her when she immigrated to the United States in 1988 at eighteen years old with her mother and new American stepfather. Remembering the importance of education ingrained in her from her uncle, Kathleen went on to study political science at the University of West Florida. After receiving her master's degree, she planned to continue her education at the doctoral level and pursue a career in academia. She had already, by this time, incurred an enormous amount of student loan debt, prompting her to consider ways to pay off her loans before beginning her PhD program. When a friend—a Naval Academy graduate—offered to pass along her résumé to some contacts in the Washington metro area, Kathleen obliged, not knowing exactly where it would lead.

Months later, Kathleen received an offer of employment from the CIA, and without hesitation, she accepted. She took on the challenge, embracing it fully, never doubting her ability to do it. It would be years before Kathleen would realize how much her uncle influenced that life-altering decision. Of course, she had her trepidations, and the security investigation certainly wasn't the smoothest or fastest process. The Agency is diligent about tracking down every foreign national contact a person has—so you can imagine how complicated the process would be for a woman who spent the first eighteen years of her life overseas. And her polygraph? Kathleen would later describe it as "very unpleasant," but like many who had gone before and continued after her, it wasn't enough to discourage her from joining the organization.

What Kathleen intended as a "stopgap measure" lasting three to five years—just enough time to pay back some of her student loans—turned into something else entirely when she learned how enticing the role of an operations officer was. And one simple meet-cute in the office with another operations officer sealed the deal for her. Kathleen had found herself a long-term career and a pretty exciting one at that.

Kathleen had just returned from a TDY in Europe when she popped into a friend's office to say hi one spring day in late May 1997, just a year after she started at the Agency. That's when Joe spotted her. At only twenty-seven years old, Kathleen could easily pass for younger, so it wasn't necessarily surprising when Joe mistook her for a new college intern or "a Summer Only," especially given the time of year. He vowed to keep his distance, assuming the age gap and life stage were drastically too different, but when he discovered that she was in fact an officer, all bets were off. Joe devised a ploy to get Kathleen's attention—he set up a time to talk to her about all things East Asia to prepare him for his upcoming tour there. It didn't occur to Kathleen that Joe might be interested in her. Blond-haired and blue-eyed at five eleven with a muscular build, he wasn't the type of man she usually went for. And so, when he asked her out for a beer, she assumed it was to talk more about work, and the thought that they could be a good match was far from her mind.

Like any good operations officer, Joe wooed Kathleen with his variety of interests, and his happened to be particularly fascinating. Prior to his Agency career, he was an archaeologist, having lived with a Stone Age tribe in the Philippines—a real-life Indiana Jones turned James Bond. Joe shared his interest in writing a book with Kathleen, and she was taken by how intelligent, generous, and eager this man was. As Kathleen began to consider dating Joe, she couldn't help but think of his imminent departure to East Asia in just three short months.

"Okay, we can date," she told him. "But you're leaving so soon, so let's just see how it goes."

But the moment Kathleen started seeing Joe as a prospective partner, everything changed for her. Over the next three months, they spent virtually every day together. There was something about his personality and his positive approach to life that drew her to him. They were inseparable. Soon, September rolled around, and Joe was preparing to pack out for his three-year tour in East Asia.

It didn't occur to Kathleen that she would go with him—after all, you needed to be married to be on another officer's PCS orders, and they had been dating for only three months. But when he showed up one evening at her apartment in Northern Virginia and knelt next to her futon with a green twisty tie from a loaf of bread, she said yes.

One of the first people Kathleen called was her uncle.

"I've been dating this fantastic man, and he just proposed to me. I've said yes!" she told Yonghwa over the phone.

"I'm happy for you, but this is quite soon after only three months of dating, don't you think? Marriage is a lifetime commitment," he reminded her. Yonghwa was a Christian and didn't believe in divorce. How could he be sure that Kathleen wasn't making a terrible mistake? There was only one way to know for sure. He would fly to Virginia to meet Joe himself.

Just before Joe's PCS departure, Yonghwa arrived stateside to conduct his very own interview to ensure that this "fantastic man" Kathleen had described was indeed a good match for his niece. Joe passed with flying colors.

"He's a sound young man, and I can see how committed the two of you are to each other," he told Kathleen.

While she was relieved to hear this, the reality was that Kathleen had already decided she would marry Joe, regardless of what her uncle thought. Besides, he's the one who taught her to think independently, right?

Even so, Kathleen and Joe decided they'd wait to marry until after Joe's tour, even if that meant spending their engagement on opposite sides of the world. They lasted only three months. Long before the days of FaceTime and Zoom, their only way of communicating was through email, and they found the distance intolerable. Kathleen begged her manager to send her TDY to Joe's field station, and he said yes. It turned out there was legitimate work for her to do there, so it wasn't entirely a boondoggle.

While visiting Joe in the field, they decided they didn't want to wait any longer. They married right away at the local city hall equivalent and took the paperwork to the American Civil Services so the Agency would issue her PCS orders. This was November 1997, and by January the following year, headquarters created a position for Kathleen where Joe was posted in East Asia. Much like Mary and Alex, they were an official Agency "tandem couple."

This first tour for Kathleen in East Asia came with challenges—and not just the typical ones of a first-tour officer. Like Mary, Kathleen was learning those unspoken rules for female operations officers. She became attuned to the general perception that women only worked at the Agency until they got married, and in terms of performance overseas, Kathleen found that generally, the expectations for female officers' productivity were lower. The belief was that women just wouldn't do as well as their male counterparts. She found the whole atmosphere unhealthy and stifling; these biases against women infected every part of the workplace, she told me—even the lunchroom.

"Oh, Kathleen, don't stand so close to the microwave with your stomach exposed to it. It will affect your reproductive system," her male COS told her one day.

All she could do was tell him, "Thank you." This was the norm, after all. But interestingly, she found some of the most egregious examples of discrimination came from female operations officers with more seniority.

"I know your husband is also a case officer. What are his aspirations and how would your aspirations fit into his?" one senior female operations officer asked her. It didn't take long for Kathleen to realize that senior officers, especially women, viewed Joe's career as primary and hers, secondary. But Kathleen's initial hurdles weren't only related to her being a woman. It was even more complex, given that she was an Asian American woman stationed in East Asia, catering to day-to-day trials that, at times, felt stressful and exhausting.

"I don't think you're supposed to come into this vault," an embassy officer said to Kathleen, mistaking her for a Foreign Service National (FSN), a local citizen working at a US Embassy where she had a meeting. It wasn't the first time this happened to her, and she knew it wouldn't be the last.

"I could have disabused them right then and there, and said, 'I'm an American, etc.' instead of brooding," Kathleen would lament to me years later. She'd need a few more tours under her belt before she would learn to stand up for herself in those instances. To make matters even more difficult, Kathleen and Joe faced discrimination for their interracial marriage on a regular basis. It didn't help that many of the male officers at Station and in other US-run facilities had local girlfriends who didn't always have the best reputations. Some nights, after a long day at work, Kathleen would return to her home only to have to show her badge and convince the security guard that she wasn't a barmaid walking the streets at night; she was the woman of the house.

It wasn't just the discrimination against *women* that came to light in the Glass Ceiling study in 1991. It also uncovered deeply rooted institutional bias and discrimination against minorities, including Asian Americans. Indeed, despite constituting about 10 percent of the professional workforce, minorities—including men and women who identified as Asian Pacific American, Black, Hispanic, or Native American—only held 4 percent of the SIS positions. Asian Americans specifically, accounted for less than 2 percent. The bias was so extreme that the top eleven Agency executives interviewed in the study said that one possible reason white males have traditionally been given career-making assignments in the Agency could be because "women and minorities may suffer from 'risk aversion'—a reluctance to try new and different tasks or jobs." The study speculated even further, saying it may actually be the managers who are "reluctant to promote women or minorities for fear that the person might fail or not do as well in the new endeavor."

The study also found data that supported stereotyping of minorities, noting an extremely high percentage of foreign-born Asian Pacific Americans who reported using foreign language skills at 51 percent as compared to 30 percent or fewer of the other groups, including US-born Asian Pacific Americans. Individuals in focus groups even voiced the stereotype that minorities have trouble with writing and oral skills—something that Kathleen took pains to master, acutely aware of her immigrant status and how it may impact others' perceptions of her.

Despite some challenges as both a woman and a minority, Kathleen forged ahead as best she could, working hard to establish herself in the world of international espionage. Her first operational meetings in the field were nerve-racking yet exciting. She spent hours brainstorming with her husband and colleagues before each one, especially during her first six months, game-planning out each scenario: "If the asset says this, what do I say?" She'd also familiarize herself with all the potential counterintelligence implications to be sure she understood what she could and couldn't say.

Her overpreparation stemmed from more than being a first-time officer. Kathleen never forgot that she was a late immigrant to the United States; it was always playing in the back of her mind. As a result, she worked even harder, putting an intense amount of pressure on herself. She ensured her cables and intelligence reports required minimal editing, if at all, and when she talked to her peers about her cases, she made sure her English was as error-proof as possible.

Kathleen handled a variety of cases during her first tour, and some of the trickiest ones were the relationships with liaison, the host country's intelligence service. For those meetings, Kathleen prepared all her formal agenda items. For others, she could dangle her connections to the American community as an entrée to a conversation and then use her cultural background, age, and interests to build rapport; business didn't have to come first. For all targets, she considered questions like: *What makes him tick? What does he like to do? And just as important, how can I create a personal relationship with him without him misinterpreting my intentions as romantic?* She learned from her very first meeting to set a boundary in a way that was official, professional, and friendly, because it was important that they like her.

Having the right balance was crucial because the relationship they were creating was one of exclusivity. Her male assets were telling her things they didn't even tell their spouses. Moreover, such assets often have other issues, like substance abuse or psychological hang-ups, so it was key that she delicately revisit these boundaries even after recruitment all while protecting the assets' ego and giving them a sense of stability and security. She had to be attuned to her verbal and nonverbal cues because if she made a mistake, she knew it would end up on the front page of *The Washington Post*.

But Kathleen didn't make a mistake. By all accounts, she had a successful first tour, even if she *was* exhausted from the artificial barriers and microaggressions she dealt with day in and day out as an Asian American woman on a tour in East Asia. She couldn't help but feel that these difficulties kept her from having more successful operations. As the nineties came to a close for Kathleen and she prepared for her next tour, she was unsure about this new career in espionage and whether she had what it took to be an operations officer. She'd soon find out.

NAME: DENISE
YEAR OF BIRTH: 1970
PLACE OF BIRTH: NORTHERN VIRGINIA
ENTRANCE ON DUTY: 1990
FIELD TRADECRAFT CERTIFICATION: YES (But not yet)

HOME BASE: AFRICA DIVISION
FOREIGN LANGUAGE: FRENCH

While Mary and Kathleen, both recent college graduates, were beginning their first careers at CIA in the mid-nineties, Denise, a nineteen-year-old with a high school diploma, was earning her chops as a secretary. Denise's upbringing was what you'd consider traditional: the stay-at-home mom and the working dad who didn't carry his weight when it came to domestic responsibilities. What wasn't traditional, however, was that Denise grew up largely overseas because her father was a communications officer for the CIA. Bouncing from continent to continent during her formative years, Denise got a taste for what it's like to live overseas from a young age, and those experiences shaped her, but even so, Denise didn't set out to work at the CIA. In fact, she once thought she'd pursue a career related to the arts. She participated in international honor choir and even had several choir solos in high school. But when her parents learned of her creative ambitions, they steered her to what they viewed as a more practical path. It was important to Denise's parents that she be the first in their blue-collar family to get a bachelor's degree, and when she wasn't interested in applying to college, her mother filled out the applications for her.

Denise lasted six months at college. It wasn't that she didn't have a good work ethic—she did. (In fact, her work ethic and commitment to the mission would become one of her strongest traits and keys to success at the CIA in the years to come.) But only if it interested her. And it's safe to say that being locked in a classroom didn't. So, she stopped showing up for class and ultimately flunked out. When Denise found herself on a plane back home to her parents' house at an overseas location for her father's latest field assignment, she wasn't met with open arms at the airport; her parents didn't even pick her up. With all of her belongings stuffed in three suitcases, she had to find her way home on her own.

"What are you gonna do with your life?" her dad asked once she arrived.

"I don't know . . . I'm nineteen, I'll get a job at the shoppette," she told him, referring to the convenience store on the local military base.

"You're gonna pay me $240 a month in rent," he said.

"Wait, you're in government housing."

"That's none of your business; you're gonna pay rent. Can you type?"

She could. In fact, she did pretty well at typing in high school. And so, Denise's father had her fill out the thirty-seven-page application by hand in a controlled space at the local CIA field station. He triple-wrapped it and sent it manually back to Langley. It turned out, there was a shortage on secretaries, and in September 1990, Denise entered on duty as a secretarial trainee at the equivalent of a GS-5 in a technical office that her father had worked in for years.

It wasn't just the experience of a childhood growing up overseas with a CIA-employed father that prepared Denise for work in espionage. There were mental health challenges and relationship dynamics at home with her parents that led her to take more of an adult role at a young age. It was those experiences that hardened her in a way that protected her from the types of discrimination she would face as a woman at the CIA. And she did face it. One man, for example, made a habit of grabbing her breasts every time he saw her while saying, "Honk!" When she took the issue to HR, a woman named Nancy discouraged her from filing an official complaint.

"Oh, he's so close to retiring. He's only got three more months left. You don't want to ruin his career. It's only a few more months.

By the time they investigate, you're going to look like the troublemaker. You don't want to be *that* girl." Nancy was nearly sixty years old and had been around a long time—this was 1991.

From then on, when Denise saw him in the hallway, she preempted his advances by calling out loudly, "Don't you fucking touch me!" She felt her only defense was either embarrassing him or avoiding him all together. She established that no one was going to mess with her. She was a force to be reckoned with, and it was clear even then to those around her that there was no stopping her. In addition to her secretarial duties, Denise was doing what felt like a hundred other things (and probably was pretty close to that), volunteering outside of her sphere and constantly looking for ways to learn new skills.

By the end of the nineties, Denise had done one tour in Europe as a secretary and topped out at a GS-9. She could go into human resources and work her way up to a GS-13, but she always dreamed of living in Africa, so she applied for a job as an executive secretary in the Africa front office in the DO and got it. Denise continued to fill her time with various side hustles like typing out her boss's notes that he wrote in longhand on yellow legal pads. Every time she volunteered to do something for someone, she learned something new. And soon, she learned about the role of support officer for the DO. In this role, she would no longer be limited to secretarial work—she would handle vouchers, accountings, and logistics, among other duties. Although she wouldn't be an operations officer, she might even be asked to help with a little operational support. And so, as the nineties came to a close, Denise transitioned to a support officer in Africa Division, where she would continue to inch closer and closer to running her own clandestine operations.

Mary's and Kathleen's experiences as female operations officers who came on board in the nineties are emblematic of the types of issues women were dealing with in the DO during this time. Their experiences were made exceptionally unique and complex given that they were both first-generation immigrants, which worked to their benefit in some circumstances but also came with its own set of challenges. While Denise's experience coming into the CIA as a secretary was different, she, too, encountered some discrimination as a woman. Like Mary, Kathleen, and so many others, Denise didn't let that stop her from advancing through the ranks. What the women—or men, for that matter—didn't know was that the start of the next decade would bring with it an event that would change the world and intelligence collection as they knew it. Priorities would shift, which meant more opportunities for women and far less time to waste on doubting their abilities.

CHAPTER 5

THE TERRORISM-
DRIVEN 2000s

The year 2000 ushered in a decade full of opportunities and growth for women both in and outside of the CIA. At the start of the decade, there were only two female CEOs of Fortune 500 companies, and by the end, there were fifteen. And in 2009, Ursula Burns became the first Black woman CEO of a Fortune 500 company.[1] Meanwhile, the media was busy tearing down the very pop icons it had spent the nineties building up. Diane Sawyer's and Matt Lauer's interviews of Britney Spears, for example, openly questioned her sex life and slut-shamed her.[2,3] "What happened to your clothes?" Sawyer asked her of a recent photoshoot in *Esquire*, no attempt at hiding the judgment in her voice.[4]

The Bond franchise, however, continued its trajectory of strong, complex female roles into the 2000s with Broccoli leading the charge. The films boasted more developed female characters like Jinx (Halle Berry) in *Die Another Day* and Vesper Lynd (Eva Green) in 2006's *Casino Royale*. (I saw the latter in the theater with some close friends who were unaware that in just a few short weeks, I'd be reporting for duty for *my* new top secret career at the CIA.) And the role of "M" was now played by a woman, Judi Dench. By the end of the decade, Daniel Craig had won audiences over as a new, grittier Bond coupled with the strongest female portrayals yet.

Meanwhile, the CIA was grappling with the new War on Terror after the devastating attacks on September 11, 2001, when nineteen al-Qaeda terrorists hijacked four commercial passenger planes and flew them into the World Trade Center Twin Towers, the Pentagon, and a field in rural Pennsylvania. In the wake of the attacks, the Agency was deciphering what intelligence collection looked like in a post-9/11 world. The intelligence community, built around the decades-long threat from the Soviet Union and bursting with Cold War experts, was suddenly facing a new kind of threat—one it found it was ill-prepared to combat. It began recruiting new employees, especially Arabic speakers, at a record pace, essentially rebuilding itself after severe budget cuts and government hiring freezes in the 1990s under the Clinton administration. The CIA's priorities had shifted to counterterrorism, almost exclusively. At the time of 9/11, the Counterterrorism Center (CTC) was a tiny subset of NE Division, nothing like the enormous entity it would become over the next fifteen years.

"CTC was such a backwater. I mean the whole counterterrorism mission was not taken seriously until after 9/11," said Gina Bennett, a former CIA counterterrorism analyst who spent thirty-four years at the Agency.[5] "Honestly, in CTC, there were already a lot of women in the counterterrorism mission, and I believe a lot of that has to do with the fact that it *was* a backwater mission."

Bennett attributes the large number of women in CTC to the fact that it was much more common to find male analysts in regional offices where there were more opportunities to write fast-breaking intelligence articles for the President's Daily Brief and advance their careers. Similarly, CIA officers in the DO had long been uninterested in CTC; Bennett noted that part of that stemmed from a lack of cable releasing authorities until Alec Station, the standalone unit dedicated to tracking Osama bin Laden, was created in 1996.

The 1998 embassy bombings in Dar es Salaam and Nairobi planted the seeds of change, but it wasn't until 9/11 that change really took hold. This shift in priorities to counterterrorism meant female analysts in CTC were finally taken more seriously,[6] and the new war zone tour requirement gave operations officers a similar experience and equal footing right off the bat, which helped normalize women serving in the most difficult environments and the idea that men and women could serve side by side.[7] That shift didn't change everything overnight though; retail outlets didn't even have appropriate war zone attire in women's sizes.

"REI only had hot pink ski gear. I had to buy teenage boy sizes," one technical operations officer told me about shopping for the items in her kit to deploy to the war zone. "There weren't even clothes on the market for us." President George W. Bush would later call her "the hottest counterterrorism analyst he'd ever seen."[8]

Even so, the all-hands-on-deck mentality meant more opportunities for women to shine—women like Mary, Kathleen, and Denise, who played key roles in meeting and recruiting assets to collect foreign intelligence, including terrorist threats, all in an effort to keep America and Americans abroad safe.

Mary

Mary was a year into her second field tour at an undisclosed location, which allowed her and Alex to be near his mother, who had recently taken a nasty fall down the stairs. Early into the tour, Mary became pregnant, and in 2000, she gave birth to a daughter, whom they named Layla. Prior to the birth, Mary had been developing a source from an Arab country, and when Layla was only a few weeks old, the source reached out to say he was interested in getting his son's US citizenship, which told Mary he was prime for recruitment. But when she looked down at Layla, so fresh and tiny in her BabyBjörn strapped to her chest, Mary remembered the commitment she made to be there for her newborn—especially during those first three months. And so, she gave the source instructions to arrive at a restaurant down the street the following Monday and turned the case over to her husband. Alex ended up recruiting him, as Mary expected, and when headquarters sent a kudos cable weeks later, it acknowledged her hard work on the case. It may have been the first, but it wouldn't be the last time Mary was faced with choices when it came to motherhood and her career.

Mary planned to stay in this undisclosed field station for a third and final year, but after 9/11, her plans changed. The Agency, equipped with plenty of Russian experts, suddenly found itself in dire need of Arabic speakers, which meant Mary's skill set and background was in even higher demand. After all, there weren't many female operations officers in general, let alone with her abilities. When her current deputy chief of station was assigned to an Arab country for his next tour, there was a position for Mary (and her husband) there to use her operational skills and Arab expertise to make significant contributions to the mission and in the fight against al-Qaeda.

Over the next year, Mary handled several cases, even some that ventured into the more technical sphere, which didn't scare her, because she had always excelled at math and science in school. She was pregnant with their second child at this time, but that didn't slow her down. In mid-2002, she returned to the

States for access to better medical care to give birth to a son named Michael. She returned to Station a few months later, hitting the ground running with a sensitive case that required her to travel. While away, she received a troubling call from Alex, who was back in-country with Layla, now two years old, and their newborn son.

"When you get back, you'll have twenty-four hours to pack up you and the kids. We're sending you back to the US." Alex wasn't able to elaborate over an open telephone line, so Mary didn't learn until she returned to Station that they received intelligence from a credible source that another Arab country, a sworn enemy of the US, was inquiring about the defense attaché by position, the chief of station by name, and Mary, by name. It became more alarming when they stopped asking about the two men and focused solely on Mary, even attempting to gain access to blueprints of her home. When Mary arrived back at Station, she quickly packed up everything she and the kids would need, and they returned to the US, leaving Alex behind to finish his tour solo. Mary and the kids stayed with her parents at their home in Vienna, Virginia, and she returned to work at headquarters. When the PEMS officer realized Mary was back, she asked her to go on a one-year unaccompanied war zone tour to Iraq. (PEMS stood for personnel evaluations management staff and was the office that made assignments in the divisions, including overseas positions. A division's PEMS officer was considered very powerful.) Of the five women PEMS asked, two of them were nursing, including Mary. The PEMS officer didn't have children, and Mary got the sense that she harbored some sort of bitterness over it, resulting in a lack of empathy for mothers in the workplace.

"I've been asked to go to Iraq, and if it's okay with you, I'd like to turn it down. Instead, I'd like to be acting branch chief," Mary said to the chief/NE Division, whom she knew as a COS from a previous tour. The branch chief position of the country she was offering to do wasn't an easy one; in fact, it was extremely taxing, but it was at headquarters, and Mary had the support she needed at home and childcare to allow her to do it. The chief knew she wasn't shirking responsibilities, since the position would undoubtedly be a lot of work, and so he agreed. That's how Mary found herself acting branch chief fairly early in her career.

Alex completed the remainder of his tour the following year, and when he returned to headquarters, he was offered a position as chief of operations (COPS) at another NE Station. Mary was offered a position there as a line operations officer.

"We've been around long enough that I know a man is going to go further than a woman," Mary told her husband. "In looking at our next several assignments, I think we need to put your career ahead of mine. I need to take a back seat to take care of the kids. When we get back to headquarters, it will be my turn to be out in front, so you need to give me that."

Her decision was more a reflection of the current reality, rather than any sort of opting out on her part. And so, they packed up their family and went back overseas. Mary veered even more into technical collection on this tour, including one very demanding case that she traveled to the Far East to recruit. It was the first recruitment pitch that Mary wasn't 100 percent sure he would say yes. Well, she *was* sure—until she saw fear in his eyes and his knuckles turn white as his fingers gripped the chair. But thankfully, he did say yes. Mary brought him on board and trained him, and ultimately sent him into a denied area where there was no CIA physical presence. The asset more than delivered and would remain one of the cases Mary is most proud of years later after retiring from the Agency, although she'll never be able to share exactly what he collected or the specifics about the significant impact he had on national security.

While Mary's spouse's career was taking the lead on this particular tour—he was senior to her in the COPS role—she wasn't slowing down her operational tempo. She was, however, seeking ways to find more balance for her family while continuing to advance in her career. Her cases were requiring her to travel so much that when she returned to Station, she wanted to spend as much time as possible with her kids.

"Look, I'm traveling all the time, and I cannot come back and be in the office eight hours a day. I'm not seeing the kids," she told her COS. "How about I work six-hour days instead? If I drop on my productivity, then we can revisit this arrangement, but otherwise, this is what I'd like to do."

"This is great. Let's do it," he said. Mary's work didn't suffer. In fact, she even secured another recruitment on that tour. Notwithstanding, Mary never allowed herself to forget that as a woman, she had to handle herself a bit differently than her male colleagues running operations. She regularly met with an asset while driving around. On one particular evening, just before Mary dropped the asset off, she told him she was traveling to Mykonos for a family vacation.

"Can I bring anything back for you?" It was a customary question to ask an asset when traveling.

"A picture of you in a bikini," he responded.

Mary was caught off guard. That wasn't the type of relationship the two of them had, so it was unexpected, to say the least. She laughed it off but found it interesting, if not a little disturbing, that even as she was excelling and kicking ass operationally, she still faced circumstances in which she was objectified.

On her next tour, Mary stayed part-time, juggling her career as a line operations officer with motherhood while her husband took a position as the deputy chief of station in another Arab country. This time, the Station was a black site, meaning it wasn't formally acknowledged even within the walls of CIA. The hope was that Mary could use her Middle Eastern roots to break into a key inner circle of the political elites. When she arrived at the decrepit old villa that housed the covert CIA Station, she noticed how close it was to the road, a clear security concern, making it vulnerable to a terrorist attack. She stopped short of walking into the front door when Alex asked if something was wrong.

"Something bad is going to happen here. I can feel it," she told him. Months later, Mary was at the American school having coffee with other moms before she planned to go into Station late morning. Many of her children's friends came from elite families—including several with direct ties to the leader of the country where they were stationed—which meant Mary could be engaged in her children's lives while also furthering her operational goal to infiltrate the inner circle. On that particular morning, Mary planned to arrive at Station by ten. She circled the building several times, and when she still couldn't find parking, she decided to park her Nissan Xterra outside the front door of the villa on the curb—the same Nissan Xterra she and Alex had taken on previous tours. *Try to tow me. I'm an American*, she thought to herself.

Not long after, Mary was sitting at her desk just outside of Alex's office when the first grenade hit. Station leadership had procured Kevlar vests and helmets in case of attack, so they got those out along with the weapons from the safe. Mary, donning a heavy Kevlar vest and helmet, low crawled around Station, pulling out computer hard drives and putting them in the safe in case the building was overrun. She looked over to see the chief's wife, Nicole, hyperventilating.

"Hey, hey, look at me!" Mary told her. "We are walking out of here alive. Do you understand me? We are walking out of here alive. Now breathe."

And then, over the PA system, they heard the guard. "Security! Where are you?" There was no mistaking the fear and uncertainty in his voice, and that got Nicole hyperventilating again. It was clear something had gone very wrong.

"Look at me. We either walk out of here alive, or they don't take us alive," Mary said. September 11 was imprinted on her mind, and the last thing she was going to allow was for them to use her as a terror weapon against her own population. After twenty minutes, the sound of grenades and automatic gunfire dissipated. Mary wondered if they were headed to the school where her kids were. She couldn't breathe at the thought of it. *Are they going after my kids?* Mary made the quick decision to send Nicole to tell the nanny to pick up all of the kids and called her father to tell him what was going on and that if something happened to all of the parents, he should take the children back to the States with the nanny. Then she called her sister. It went to the answering machine; it was early in the morning back home.

"Hi, we're under attack. If I don't make it, I love you," she said her goodbyes. And then, Alex came out with good news.

"The guard forces have repelled the attackers. They're all dead. But one of them was driving a VBIED [vehicle-borne improvised explosive device], and it's at the back gate, and it's unexploded," Alex told the officers.

Apparently, the attacker drove into the back gate and somehow dropped the remote before detonating it. When he bent down to try to find it, he was fired on by security forces and killed. If he had been successful in detonating the bomb, it would have leveled the whole building. Security footage later showed the attackers had been casing the building and planned a multi-vehicle attack—the truck at the back gate along with three additional vehicles at the front, which planned to breach the front door. But on that particular morning, one operations officer who was coming in late after a meeting at her children's school parked right outside the front door, thwarting their perfectly laid plans.

Mary's bullet-ridden Nissan Xterra was still parked in front, having taken two hundred automatic rounds—everything but two windows had been shot out—and it had one good tire left. Mary and Alex's friends and family may have not known the location of their current overseas tour before the attack, but they did now. Once they saw the news coverage, Mary started receiving calls from friends and family all over the world, asking if they were okay.

Following the attack, Alex scraped blood, guts, and brain matter of the attackers off the concrete and put them into Ziploc bags. He placed the bags in the Station freezer, where they would stay, next to officers' microwavable frozen dinners, for the next several weeks until the FBI could retrieve them for its investigation.

Six weeks later, Mary still couldn't shake the feeling that the senior US officials weren't taking the attack seriously enough. She knew if the attackers had targeted the school, her children likely wouldn't have survived.

"We're in a police state. How does something like this happen when there's so much security? I don't want to say they condoned it, but something doesn't strike me as right," she told Alex. She proposed that she take the kids back to the US a few months early while Alex finished his tour. Their plan was to return to headquarters when this tour ended in the spring anyway, and the children's safety simply accelerated that plan. Even so, it wasn't an easy decision. Mary had made friendships there with some of the locals, one of whom had become like a sister to her. Leaving meant she couldn't speak to her again, something Mary would lament even years later after retiring from the Agency.

Mary and the kids, along with their faithful Nissan Xterra, which was good as new after paying $4,000 to a local mechanic,

Lucy Kirk, just after beginning
her career at the CIA in 1967.
Courtesy of Lucille Kirk.

cy Kirk, visiting London for
Ascot Races during a CIA field tour
a European station, 1998.
urtesy of Lucille Kirk.

Lucy Kirk, on vacation
in Sanibel Island, Florida, 1980.
Courtesy of Lucille Kirk.

Lucy Kirk in Egypt, 199
Courtesy of Lucille Kir

Lucy Kirk, 2020.
Courtesy of Lucille Kirk.

Janine Brookner, 1958.
Courtesy of the estate of Janine Brookner.

Janine Brookner on a hotel balcony
in Hong Kong while visiting her mother
and stepfather during her field tour
in East Asia in 1971.
Courtesy of the estate of Janine Brookner.

Janine Brookner in front of Colin Thompson's house in East Asia, 1972.
Courtesy of the estate of Janine Brookner.

Janine Brookner and Colin Thompson's wedding ceremony
with a Thai village chief presiding, Bangkok, 1973.
Courtesy of the estate of Janine Brookner.

Janine Brookner and Colin Thompson at their wedding reception in Bangkok, 1973. *Courtesy of the estate of Janine Brookner.*

Janine Brookner in Phnom Penh Cambodia while visiting her husband Colin Thompson, who was on extended TDY from Bangkok in 1974 *Courtesy of the estate of Janine Brookner*

Janine Brookner and her sister, Judy, on a birdwatching trip in Costa Rica, 1995. *Courtesy of the estate of Janine Brookner.*

Janine Brookner and her Maltese, Oliver, at her home in Georgetown, 2014. *Courtesy of the estate of Janine Brookner.*

Martha Peterson and John Peterson at their wedding in Fort Lauderdale, Florida on December 26, 1969. *Courtesy of Martha Peterson.*

Sketch of drop site in Moscow. *Courtesy of Martha Peterson.*

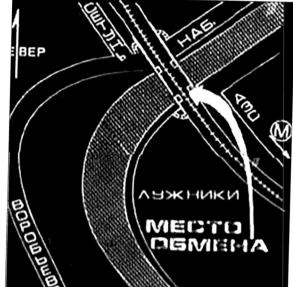

Martha Peterson's orange Zhiguli,
a Soviet-made four-cylinder Fiat sedan
that she drove in Moscow.
Courtesy of Martha Peterson.

Alexandr Dmitryevich Ogorodnik,
the Soviet agent code-named TRIGON,
for whom Marti conducted dead drops
in Moscow, including a suicide pill
disguised as a pen.
Courtesy of Martha Peterson.

Martha Peterson (bottom right) at a US Embassy party in Moscow, 1977. *Courtesy of Martha Peterson.*

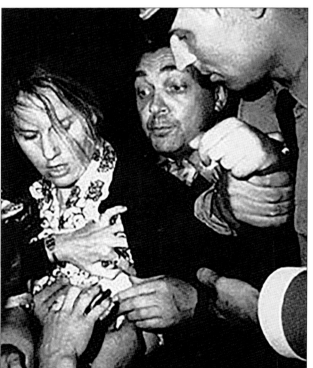

The KGB attempting to remove the SRR-100 device attached to Martha Peterson's bra with Velcro during her arrest in Moscow on July 15, 1977. *Courtesy of Martha Peterson.*

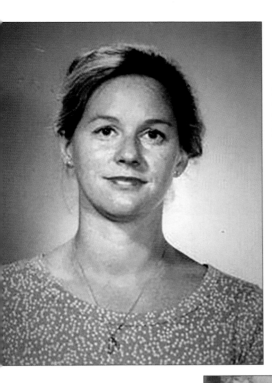

Martha Peterson's CIA badge photo taken on July 18, 1977 at CIA headquarters after she was declared persona non grata by Russia. *Courtesy of Martha Peterson.*

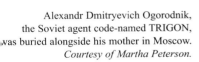

Alexandr Dmitryevich Ogorodnik, the Soviet agent code-named TRIGON, was buried alongside his mother in Moscow. *Courtesy of Martha Peterson.*

Martha Peterson, 2011.
Courtesy of Martha Peterson.

Carmen Medina in a helicopter in Iraq.
Courtesy of Carmen Medina.

Carmen Medina on the tarmac at the Kabul airport.
Courtesy of Carmen Medina.

Kathleen, while working for the CIA in Europe.
Courtesy of Kathleen.

Laura Thomas, on a personal vacation to Wadi Rum, Jordan in 2015 during her time at the CIA.
Courtesy of Laura Thomas.

moved into a home in Vienna, Virginia. Soon after, Alex joined them. She spent the next two years working in CTC full-time, and the kids were enrolled in school. She was even promoted to GS-15 at that time, no small feat for any operations officer, but Mary knew it was especially rare for a female operations officer to achieve. Everything seemed to be falling into place until one day when Alex came home and said he was offered a deputy chief position at a station in the Middle East—coincidentally in the very same station where they served their first overseas tour. At this time, the Agency was becoming stricter about nepotism, which meant it was necessary for Mary to find a position in-country that didn't report to her husband. The nature of the location and priorities there meant it was possible. All was well until about a year into their tour when Station received a threat to Mary's physical safety from a terrorist organization seeking to lure her somewhere so they could watch her more closely.

Over the next two weeks, Mary had someone armed with her at all times, and she was driven around in an armored vehicle. *I love this tour. I love this apartment. I don't want to leave,* Mary thought one night when she awoke at midnight. But she knew it was inevitable. The Agency doesn't use officers as bait, and it was no longer safe for her there. When she learned the terrorist group and their state-sponsored backers were asking about her family in Lebanon and her pregnant sister and her young children back in the States, she knew it was serious. She and the kids needed to get out of there right away. But how could they get her out without tipping their hand that they knew about the threat and revealing their sources?

A senior Agency officer happened to be visiting the country, and his executive assistant (EA) asked him to fly Mary and her two children back to the US on his plane. He said yes. That gave Station more time to ensure their sources and methods weren't blown and allowing Mary and the kids a safe return to

Washington, DC, where they would finish the decade without Alex.[9]

Kathleen

Kathleen, like Mary, experienced the sudden and extreme shift in intelligence priorities after 9/11. She was on a tour at an undisclosed field station, where she was focused on recruiting hard targets, but now she—and everyone else—was looking for counterterrorism targets. While the counterintelligence hard targets remained important, resources were largely devoted to counterterrorism efforts. It became all counterterrorism, all the time. The problem was that intelligence officers, and the CIA as a whole, simply didn't know who exactly they were looking for, which meant that even in their best efforts, there was ethnic profiling. Officers did things like talk to taxi drivers who looked like they may come from an Arab background and then attempt seeding-type operations—many of which never yielded any foreign intelligence. Simply put, the Agency was desperate to gain any insight into the Middle East and potential terrorist plots, so the bar for recruiting a counterterrorism target was extremely low; some would say it was nonexistent.

Three years after 9/11, Kathleen and Joe were looking for a new field tour in which they could both have positions that furthered their careers, which meant the station needed to be large enough to accommodate that. They landed on a large station in Southeast Asia, where they were both line operations officers. It was still all terrorism, all the time, which also meant constant bombings. There were officers dedicated to going after third-country targets, but almost everyone had to have a terrorism topic for their evaluation. Kathleen and Joe worked closely with local liaison, which included very competent law enforcement agencies and other US allies in the region.

Unlike the work Kathleen was doing in her tours just after 9/11 that felt disorganized and haphazard, the operational work she was doing now was actually making an impact. The Agency was becoming more mature and savvier, going after legitimate counterterrorism targets. Much of the intelligence she collected was tactical, which meant they were able to prevent further attacks and save lives.

Kathleen experienced a deep sense of reward that what she was doing mattered and had a direct impact, unlike the sometimes long, drawn-out counterintelligence hard target recruitments that took an enormous amount of time. In the latter, you wouldn't know the impact until years later, and by then, you would no longer have access to the case. But these terrorism cases, you'd know the impact right away. After one bombing, for example, Kathleen, together with Station's liaison partners, were able to collectively identify potential targets who perpetrated it and where they trained. While they couldn't prevent that bombing from occurring, liaison partners were able to retrieve evidentiary materials immediately, which led to some high-level arrests, albeit some weren't until years later. Kathleen felt like she was working in the Wild West, and she was both enjoying it and excelling in her role.[10]

In order to be successful in this type of environment, however, Kathleen had to learn to suppress her normal sensory responses to the gruesome information she would hear and see. After one bombing, she met her liaison partners at a local hotel late into the evening.

"I have something in the trunk of my car for you to see," the officer from the local security services excitedly told Kathleen.

"What is it?"

"Just come see."

"I'm not coming without knowing what it is."

"It's the head of the suicide bomber."

Kathleen knew by this point that when suicide bombers wore a vest, their extremities flew off, and the head in particular popped off like a champagne cork. In this particular case, the head was completely intact and found several meters away. The officer had it in his trunk—in a cooler, of course, to keep it safe from the sweltering heat—and was quite proud of himself. Kathleen told him she was uninterested in seeing it, but she later saw the footage they produced using the decapitated head to manipulate the image as if the person was still alive. They then circulated it as a type of wanted poster to help them gather more intelligence.

Over the course of this tour, Kathleen would continue to become desensitized to things like dead bodies and disturbing stories she'd hear from her assets. She'd experience so much of it over the coming years, in fact, that she'd later wonder, *What is it like to live normally?* But it would be several more years and tours overseas before she'd get to that point.

After her tour in Southeast Asia, Kathleen returned to headquarters for a tour in East Asia Division, during which time her spouse was surged to a war zone for a one-year unaccompanied tour. The two of them were so busy that being apart didn't affect their marriage. They saw each other every three months when Joe had a two-week R&R, and they were often in touch electronically through the Agency's secure phone line and instant message system. Kathleen knew she'd need to do a war zone tour as well, but the two opted not to do them at the same time because neither wanted to leave their two cats, whom they had grown to love and appreciate as their children.

When Joe was finishing his tour, he planned to travel home via Islamabad, where he stayed at the Marriott to enjoy a nice shower and delicious meals before wrapping up his one-year tour. Kathleen was home when she received a call from Joe.

"I'm okay," he said when she answered.

"Why shouldn't you be okay?" While Joe was dining at the hotel on the evening of September 20, 2008, a dumpster truck filled with explosives was detonated in front of the Marriott, killing at least fifty-four people. Kathleen immediately turned on the television and saw the coverage all over the news. Joe asked her to call his mother, who knew he was in that region but not that he was at that specific hotel. He worried she would see him in the news footage coming out of the wreckage and worry. Through the whole conversation with Kathleen, Joe was calm. In fact, both of them were calm. He told Kathleen that the first thing he did was look around to try to determine a possible secondary bombing—he knew terrorists often did this to maximize casualties. Joe ushered people away from the likely secondary site, all the while maintaining his calm and thinking on his feet. Kathleen thinks his personality had a lot to do with it, but the CIA's training helped him hone this ability over the years.

"The training forces you to react logically. If you react emotionally and then completely black out, during the training, you'll be counseled," she told me. "It's very interesting to see how much the training helps . . . they make it as real as possible. It opens the eyes of how you see yourself. It's not like you do it once. They put you in artificial situations a lot. If you already have it like Joe, you can hone it. If you're like me, more emotional, over time, you will yourself to react that way, and it becomes second nature."

Once Joe returned, it was Kathleen's turn to do a war zone tour. It wasn't a choice at the time—it was an expectation. A position as deputy branch chief of liaison became available, and so Kathleen checked the "management box" and thought, *Let's do it*. The Station was large with many layers. She had dealt with some of the officers before, so she had name recognition, some bona fides. When she arrived, the branch chief had to leave unexpectedly, and so they offered her the role. So many officers were coming in and out of the war zone at this time that whether you were a male or female didn't make much of a difference. After all, it wasn't even true espionage work. You were escorted to meetings by Global Response Staff (GRS), CIA officers with extensive military and/or law enforcement background who perform sensitive operations at the behest of the director worldwide. There was no secrecy surrounding who you were. Toward the end of Kathleen's tour, there was a big push in the Agency to reward people coming back from the war zone and set them up for something good—a way to sweeten the pot.

When looking at the potential options for a follow-on tour for her and Joe, the two of them had to make some decisions. As a couple without kids, they had enjoyed some flexibility over the years when it came to when and where they served. They found they were often tapped for last-minute TDYs since it was known that they didn't have kids and assumed they were available. For the most part, they didn't mind. They were dedicated to the mission, and they chose this line of work, happily in fact. On previous tours, the two of them worked hard to ensure that neither career took the lead, but when Kathleen was in Iraq, Joe had taken a very senior job at headquarters, which set him up for a senior management position overseas. That created a question of what Kathleen would do—the CIA was becoming more stringent about nepotism, which meant she wouldn't be able to work in a station where Joe was the chief or deputy.

Just at the time when Kathleen would be faced with the difficult decision of whether she should take a back seat to her husband's burgeoning career in management, the two realized he had some physical limitations stemming from the bombing in Islamabad. While he may have been medically cleared to serve overseas, he was in constant pain, which limited the amount of time he could spend in a car or on an airplane. The two decided to stay at headquarters while he went through rehabilitation, but then, instead of Joe's career taking the lead, it was Kathleen's.

The terrorist attacks Mary and Kathleen experienced in their tours were just some of the many terrorist threats to the United States, and specifically, CIA officers at the time. The most detrimental attack, however, was at Forward Operating Base Chapman, a US military base in Khost, Afghanistan, on December 30, 2009, when a double agent detonated an explosive device, blowing himself up and killing seven CIA officers and two others. Following the attack, the Agency conducted an investigation and various other "lessons learned" to discover what they could have done differently to prevent it. There were, of course, the obvious things—they could have informed the military in advance that the asset was coming, they could have stopped and searched him when he came onto base, and they could have limited the people who came out to greet him upon his arrival. Gina Bennett, who was working in CTC at the time, noted that those decisions were deemed justifiable in context, and at any particular moment, another leader on the ground may have made the same decisions.

Even so, Bennett said the criticism after the attack was aimed very squarely at Jennifer Matthews, the chief of base, who detractors blamed for not having the necessary experience to be in charge because she did the "quickie version" of the Farm and that she was "really just an analyst." And to be fair, some of that was warranted. One retired senior case officer, who was directly involved with the case, noted that while she was an expert in counterterrorism, running a base was a completely different skill set. But more than anything, Bennett believed it was easy to blame Matthews because she was a woman. People viewed her decision to have so many officers at the entrance to meet the asset as a very feminine act. The external discussion surrounding the attacks also focused on Matthews as a mother of three along with the narrative that the "war zone is no place for a girl" and that she simply shouldn't have been there because she had children. Never mind the fact that one of the other officers killed, Harold Brown Jr., also had children.

"Nobody thought twice . . . in fact, his callsign was [REDACTED], so everyone applauded him, whereas for Jennifer there was a cloud," Bennett told me.

Even Matthews's longtime female colleagues in CTC said she shouldn't have gone. Bennett was furious at the people who felt that way.

"If we all don't go to war or don't do the things we need to do because we have three kids, who's gonna do all of this? Why does gender even matter?"

The reality is that it was much too complicated to place the blame on any one person, and many of the indicators that have been found now only in hindsight were things that were in play well before the asset arrived at Khost.

"It's very difficult for people to go back to that period of time and remember how close we were to the tenth anniversary of 9/11," Bennett told me. "We were under a lot of pressure to find these two guys [Zawahiri and Bin Laden]." As a result, she believed they were operating with "outcome bias," when you're so biased and driven by one possible outcome that you become blind to other possibilities. "It's just really hard for people in hindsight to remember all of that." It's much easier, it seemed, to blame the woman.

"As women, we have a token representation in any given place, so any one mistake has disproportionate impact. It's so incredibly unfair. A guy can completely fuck up, and it won't matter anywhere near as much because there are so many more of them in positions of power," Bennett said. "If a man had made the call for all of the people to meet with the source to demonstrate that we're in it and we trust you . . . if a man had made that call, I wonder if it would have been considered brave."[11]

Denise

While Mary and Kathleen were doing their part in the Agency's global counterterrorism efforts in the Middle East and Southeast Asia, Denise's long-held dream of living in Africa came to fruition when she began a tour in West Africa as a support officer for the DO. Early into her tour, a coup d'état led to the evacuation of most of Station with the exception of the chief of station, deputy chief, a few technical officers, and Denise. She was a decent French speaker, and so Station tapped her to run operational cases and work with foreign liaison services, even though she had no operational training. Station needed her, and Denise, like always, came through and did what was necessary for the mission. She had two assets she handled independently—one was a translator with occasional reporting and the other was a money guy who helped expats get local currency more easily. Denise also helped train the host-country liaison service. By the second year of her tour, even more of Station had evacuated, and Denise and the COS were the only ones left, which meant she was doing more than dabbling in operations by this point.

Despite the security situation, Denise managed to have a great social life in West Africa. She didn't, however, expect any sort of romantic life while there. On the contrary, she expected to be single and perhaps even a bit lonely. But she was in her early thirties and didn't have any sense of urgency when it came to marriage or kids. She was so entranced by the operational work that it was easy to put a romantic life on hold. Apart from a short fling with a Marine on TDY—she steered clear of any entanglements with Marines who were stationed at the embassy—she focused on work and building friendships and community. She went out to restaurants and to the beach every weekend, at least on Sundays; she often worked six days a week.

Even several bouts with giardia and one raging case of amoebic dysentery during her tour couldn't scare Denise away from West Africa. At the end of her two years, she PCSed to a different country in the region, one she described to me as the "worst hell." Rife with tribal divisions, this country had extreme levels of poverty Denise had never experienced. People often referred to the ten-thousand-year curse on the country; they were only about a hundred years in, they'd say. It was here that Denise really started to get her operational stride. All the skills she gained in her last tour prepared her to continue to assist with operations. A neighboring country was getting a lot of attention, and the border situation was complex due to counterterrorism issues.

Denise found herself managing a group of local intelligence officers, and she was also the backup handler on four different cases. Whenever an operations officer was out of town, Denise would take the meeting. To say this was abnormal for a support officer to do would be an understatement. It was true that officers in Africa often took on more responsibility than they did in stations in other parts of the globe, but Denise's ability to handle assets and conduct operations without training and to gain the trust of both her Station colleagues and assets was both impressive and rare. By this time, her French was pretty good, and she was willing to fill in the gaps wherever Station needed her. She worked all of the time, even doing some cross-border efforts in a neighboring country where the Agency was trying to get some efforts off the ground.

Denise was good at handling African assets, but it was also difficult at times. The men believed women should be in the home caring for children, cooking, and cleaning. They didn't expect to see a woman outside of the home, and a competent woman at that, let alone an intelligence officer. She was an anomaly to them. On one particular occasion, Denise went to meet with the mayor of the capital city where she was serving to discuss an ongoing issue that Station wanted help with from the local police. She went with another case officer because she was his backup when he was out of town. While waiting for the mayor, a senior intelligence officer from the local service looked to her and said, "Oh, baby, you need to experience what a real man is. Why don't you come sit on my lap?"

It wasn't the first time Denise was hit on in Africa—she regularly fielded marriage proposals. She was a curvy, plus-size woman, which she knew was attractive to the local men. It meant she had money and could afford to eat well. What's more, she represented a visa to the United States. Denise wanted to tell him she could break him like a twig (and she could). But instead, she stood up and said she needed some air. She stepped outside the office, and her Agency colleague joined her.

"I—I can't believe he said that."

"Dude, this is not my first rodeo," she said, taking a drag off her cigarette. "They say shit like this to me all the time."

She took a breath, finished her cigarette, and went back in. Denise knew that getting through to the local security service was a combination of being able to take the hits and the sideways comments. She never held it against them that they thought differently. Now, if the comments came from inside the CIA, she had no problem putting them in their place. But even then, Denise didn't let it affect her. What she had experienced with the locals was often so horrific that any discrimination she experienced within the walls of the CIA didn't bother her.

"There's no crying in espionage. You need to get over yourself and get it done," she told me on a Zoom call one morning from her home in Virginia, a year after her retirement from the Agency. Her graying hair was pulled back in a ponytail, which she casually pointed out to me. "Sometimes I have some masculine energy. I don't remember the last time I put makeup on."

While those things may be true, I know more than anything, having worked with her years after her first tours in Africa, that it's Denise's ability to build trust with others and to leave her judgment at the door that have contributed to her successful career. And she knew she had gained the trust of the local service when they began using the French word for "he" instead of "she." They saw her as one of the guys.

Denise worked a lot of hours on this tour, like she always did, but at one point, she started feeling lonely and longed for romance. She began dating a Lebanese businessman named Yusuf who was a Canadian citizen. Ironically, in an organization that's built on secrets, you could expect absolutely zero privacy when it came to your own sex life while working at the CIA. Because he was a foreign national, Denise filled out paperwork detailing her intimate relationship with Yusuf and submitted it to her COS, who happened to be friends with him. Yusuf was wealthy, had access to a boat and a beach house, and Denise enjoyed spending time with him. She knew she wasn't his only girlfriend though, and she was under no illusions that their relationship was one that would survive in the real world. But it was just the salve she needed to get her through the lonely moments of her second West Africa tour.

Remarkably, Denise had garnered a reputation as a "one-woman CIA station" because of her ability to do nearly every job, making her virtually indispensable. Six months before her tour ended, the COS said to her, "Denise, you really have a knack for this. You should be doing ops. And you're terrible at vouchers." It was true. She hated doing finance vouchers and often let them pile up until right before the regional finance officer came to Station. Finance wasn't her joy or her passion, but dealing with Africans was. And so, when Denise returned to headquarters, she took an interim position on the desk in Africa Division, who then sponsored her to get her field trade-craft certification. She was almost twenty years into her Agency career at this point and eligible for the mid-career ops certifica-tion course that was a few weeks shorter and didn't require her to travel to the Farm. She passed with flying colors, which was no surprise given that she had already been writing cables and handling assets for years.

Operational certification in hand, Denise was ready for her first tour as a line operations officer. This time, instead of West Africa, she found herself in a small station in the Horn of Africa. She was handling cases and out on the streets, looking for intelligence targets. Unlike before, she now felt the pressure of trying to recruit an asset. After all, recruiting was a case offi-cer's bread and butter. There weren't a lot of targets, and Station was focused on counterterrorism. But Denise did everything she could think of and gave it her all—even if that meant count-less receptions in the evenings and meeting targets whenever they could meet, during work hours or after. Thankfully, it paid off, and she got the recruitment she was gunning for.

When Denise wasn't chasing after recruitment targets and handling assets, she spent time with friends from the expat community. A friend hosted a movie night one evening, and that's where she connected with Chris, a handsome history teacher from the Midwest and military reservist who planned to be in-country for four months. The two of them had spent time together in a group setting on several occasions, but it wasn't until this night that a romance began. He was smart and had a good sense of humor, and the two of them hit it off. They enjoyed snorkeling and scuba diving together—among other things. But when his tour ended, he went back to the States, and they didn't exchange contact information. Their lives were too different. Denise couldn't imagine a situation in which she would step off her career track and move to the Midwest to be with him, and he wasn't about to uproot his life as a teacher. The two appreciated what they had together and moved on.

A few weeks later, Denise learned she was pregnant. It came as a shock to her because she thought she'd never be able to conceive. She had been overweight for many years, and while back at headquarters she underwent gastric bypass surgery, leading to significant weight loss of 140 pounds and, apparently, an ability to get pregnant. In June 2009, she flew to London for a first trimester checkup—the medical care where she was stationed was admittedly subpar. Sadly, she learned at the appointment that the baby didn't have a heartbeat, and she had a D&C performed at the hospital in London. Forty-eight hours later, she was on a plane back to Station, conducting an ops meeting soon after landing.

Denise was crushed having lost the baby. And on top of that trauma, she had a new COS, who referred to women in Station as "cunts." He was a paranoid, heartless leader. Denise held it together during work hours, but after work, she sobbed. Dealing with both personal and work hardships at the same time was becoming too much to bear. She reached out to her mom, a psychiatric nurse, who recommended Denise find someone to speak to. With her mom's support and encouragement, she sought mental health treatment from an American doctor in-country.

While the pregnancy may have thrown Denise for a loop, it also made her pause and think about what she wanted at this point in her career and in life. She began having conversations with her family about the possibility of pursuing fertility treatments. She already had her next assignment in the Sahel, the vast, semiarid region of western and north-central Africa, and she knew she could afford to be a single mom. It meant she'd need to work fewer hours, but she was prepared to do that. Besides, she could be a single mom and afford household help and a nanny in the field much easier than she could in the US. She viewed raising a child overseas by herself as an opportunity to slow down, work fewer hours, and give her child an international upbringing similar to her own. And so, Denise made plans to return to the States on R&R for her first attempt at IVF a week before Christmas. The treatment was successful, and Denise became pregnant again. But three months later, she was hemorrhaging.

She lost the baby.

Denise finished out the remainder of her tour at a grueling pace, not allowing her much time to process the trauma that she had endured, and by the fall of 2010, she was back at headquarters, where she'd stay for the next year before heading back out to the field once again.

The end of the early 2000s found all three women—Mary, Kathleen, and Denise—back at headquarters. They now had multiple overseas tours under their belts and, with that, came a clear understanding of the role their gender played in clandestine operations both inside the building and in operational relationships with their assets. While the three of them offer insight into female operations officers' experiences in a post-9/11 world, their individual choices make for three unique careers at the CIA. After experiencing multiple threats to her and her family's security overseas, Mary made the decision to let her spouse's career take the lead, while she focused more of her attention on their children. Kathleen was prepared to take on more leadership roles as her husband's imminent retirement allowed for more flexibility in her own career. As for Denise, she continued to climb her way up the ranks as a single woman at the Agency who, despite the obstacles she faced, wasn't deterred. It's that same grit that would carry her through the remainder of her career when she would face more challenges ahead.

CHAPTER 6

THE GROUNDBREAKING 2010s

A mid a growing #MeToo movement, women were making key strides in multiple arenas in the 2010s: Female military officers were no longer banned from serving in combat positions, Hillary Clinton became the first woman to receive a presidential nomination from a major political party, and NASA astronauts Jessica Meir and Christina Koch made history with the first all-women spacewalk. The Bond franchise, ever changing with the times, created a new Bond Girl, Dr. Madeleine Swann, played by Léa Seydoux, whom the actress described as "not like what you can expect from a Bond Girl. . . . She's not seducing with her clothes. . . . She uses her mind."[1]

By now, women at the CIA had long been conducting their own clandestine operations, recruiting assets, and serving in war zones, but when it came to senior intelligence positions, there continued to be a drastic drop-off for women. In fact, CIA director General David H. Petraeus was so concerned by the unusually low percentage of women promoted to the senior intelligence ranks that in 2012 he asked former secretary of state Madeleine Albright to lead a study examining why more women at the CIA were "not achieving promotions and positions of greater responsibility." This study, named the Director's Advisory Group (DAG) on Women in Leadership, acknowledged women's talents and expertise as directly relevant to the success of the mission and identified multiple recommendations for CIA to course correct, including a plan to address both organizational and employee flexibility, which affect the work-life balance decisions employees make throughout their careers.[2]

While the study looked at women across the Agency, women's experiences varied according to directorate, as they often had through the decades. The DI, for example, continued to lead the way as the most progressive of the directorates. One analyst named Kate, who joined the CIA first as a college intern in 2012 and then full-time in 2017, noted that she was assigned a female mentor, a senior analyst on her team, when she first entered on duty. "I was just kind of instantly hit with, this is a place where there are a lot of women leaders, not in formal management positions, but still very much taking the leading roles."

While there *were* women, and she herself uses a wheelchair, there were no people of color on her team, women or men, so it seemed even the DI had some more work to do when it came to diversity, equity, inclusion, and accessibility (DEIA).

A DS&T officer had a vastly different experience when she began at the Agency as a mid-career hire on a male-dominated team working on data science in 2015. "The old boys' club is alive and well," she told me—referring to both then and now. She, unlike the DI analyst, was assigned a "SWAM" mentor at the start of her Agency career. (SWAM meaning straight, white, able, and male.) And like Carmen back in the seventies, she was excluded when the men all met for lunch, left alone at her desk. When she was finally invited, it felt awkward to be the only female.[3]

Although the #MeToo movement was gaining attention outside of the CIA, it hadn't quite taken hold within the halls of Langley—some would argue that the Agency's own #MeToo movement wouldn't come for another ten-plus years (don't worry; I'll get to that in the next chapter). While not officially part of the study, the DAG included a section on reinforcing the CIA's zero-tolerance policy toward gender discrimination, sexual harassment, and unlawful bias, noting that diversity and inclusion efforts cannot be successful in an environment where these behaviors occur. The study called on CIA leadership to provide safe reporting mechanisms and on witnesses to report incidents so leadership may address the incidents effectively. To say that this is easier said than done would be an understatement. After all, how do you change decades of culture with one study? Nonetheless, seeing it in black and white with Secretary Albright's name attached to it was certainly a start.[4]

Despite these challenges, women like Mary, Kathleen, and now Denise, too, had learned how to find success as female operations officers in the DO. The three of them also found that working as case officers required that they make certain choices and sacrifices, which undoubtedly determined the trajectory each of their careers took in their final years at the Agency.

Mary

Mary was adjusting to life as a single parent to her two young kids while Alex finished out his tour as deputy chief of station. She didn't want to leave Station early—by all accounts, she was having a successful tour. But the situation was such that it was simply too dangerous for her and her family, at home and abroad, if she stayed. Back in the States, Mary had the help of their nanny, which allowed her to successfully juggle the demands of her new role as chief of operations (COPS) of a fast-paced division at headquarters. She stayed in that role until Alex returned, and soon after, he took an assignment as a chief of base in a war zone. He felt strongly that he needed to give back after the Khost bombing. At the time, the Agency was offering sizable bonuses to officers who served in a war zone; Mary and Alex opted to donate that money to the CIA Officers Memorial Foundation.

After some time passed, Mary received a call one day at headquarters from the chief of staff to one of the seventh-floor principals. "You can't tell anyone I'm having this conversation with you, but he wants to know if you want to come be his EA." (She and Alex both previously applied for the executive assistant [EA] position but weren't selected.) Soon after, she was officially offered the role.

"I know your husband is in a war zone, and you're a single mom. Take the weekend to think about it," Mary recalled the chief of staff telling her. She knew the position was demanding. Similar to shadowing- and grooming-type roles in the private sector, an EA at the CIA was a prestigious role and opportunity, reserved for a select few senior officers who were chosen because they had the potential to rise to the senior leadership ranks at the Agency. The opportunity wasn't lost on Mary; she accepted the job. She served in that role for fourteen months, which she called "eye-opening" and "one of the most cohesive, best work experiences" she had ever had, due in large part to this particular leader's management style. She described him as a very inclusive manager who favored a coaching mentality over micromanaging.

"It was an amazing experience to sit up there and not just see how the sausage is made, but in addition, having that relationship with the NSC [National Security Council] and with [Capitol] Hill and other organizations within the intelligence community and Department of Defense was absolutely amazing." What's more, Mary developed such a strong relationship of trust with the principal that he often gave her the bandwidth to act on his behalf. He began to consider her his "de facto deputy chief of staff." She was privy to content and conversations at high levels that she otherwise wouldn't have been exposed to and strengthened her network, forming close relationships with the NSC and Congress. She became a substantive expert on all topics and knew exactly what levers to pull inside the organization to get things done. It was during this rotational assignment that Mary realized how far behind the DO was in terms of officers understanding how to advocate for themselves. She realized it was the *analysts*, like then–Deputy Director Michael Morrell who came up in the DI, who were in charge. Mary left this role just as Avril Haines came on board as the new deputy director. "Leave or she'll try to keep you, and that's not what you need for your career," a seventh-floor principal told her.

From there, Mary went on to take a series of leadership roles at headquarters with an eye of advancing to the SIS level. She missed the work of a line operations officer, but once her kids hit middle school, she knew she needed more stability for them. They had spent more time overseas than in the States by this point, and one of her children had mental health struggles that precluded them from moving again. That also meant a war zone tour was off the table for Mary. But going back to the DO was like going back in time. Mary felt like she didn't fit there anymore. The perspective she gained on the seventh floor meant that she thought differently now. And so, she became the assistant deputy director of operations (ADDO) for technology, where she worked across directorates to give the DO the tools it needed for officers to do their job. This was a particular interesting role at the time, given that Director John Brennan had just reorganized the Agency and added a directorate that would focus exclusively on exploiting advances in computer technology and communication, dubbed the Directorate of Digital

Innovation.[5] Mary became a key player in kicking off and then seeing through what became the DO's cloud adoption strategy. It was in this role that Mary realized her superpower is her ability to lead through influence, talk across cultures, and find ways forward. (After spending hours talking to Mary and getting to know her while researching this book, I can tell you that she is a woman with *many* superpowers.)

Mary did eventually get that SIS promotion, but in order to do so, she had to shift to the staff operations officer (SOO) career track. It had become abundantly clear to her that she wouldn't be promoted past GS-15 as a case officer. She faced the same glass ceiling Margery had identified nearly thirty years earlier when she filed the class action suit.[6]

While the DAG study noted that the career and personal choices women make can sometimes contribute to their slow career progression, it also identified the Agency's personnel management system as partially responsible for using policies and practices that can exacerbate the impact of those personal choices. In order to improve women's advancement, the study zeroed in on three critical areas: foster intentional development, value diverse paths, and increase workplace flexibility. Within those three categories, the DAG provided ten specific recommendations: (1) establish clear promotion criteria from GS-15 to SIS, (2) expand the pool of nominees for promotion to SIS, (3) provide relevant demographic data to panels, (4) establish equity assurance representative role on panels, (5) reduce and streamline career development tools, (6) create an on-ramping program, (7) provide actionable and timely feedback to all employees, (8) develop future leaders, (9) unlock talent through workplace flexibility, and (10) promote sponsorship.

One of the obstacles to promotion the study highlighted was the importance the Agency placed on "extreme jobs." Indeed, since 9/11, the pressure for officers to complete a war zone tour wasn't just encouraged in the DO; it was a requirement in order to progress in your career. But as the study noted, women were less likely to take jobs with long or unpredictable hours in part because "women tend to feel the impact and 'opportunity cost' of an extreme job at home more so than men." Take Mary for example, who at this point in her career opted to prioritize the health and stability of her children over a war zone tour. As a result, she served in roles that significantly broadened her view of the intelligence community and equipped her with an array of new skills. Similarly, the DAG encouraged the Agency to "think more broadly about how experiences derived from one extreme job could be gained from a combination of several positions over a longer period of time," and Mary's experience was testament to that approach.[7] And yet she was forced to switch career tracks in order to reach the SIS ranks due to the expectations, some written and some implicit, to be competitive for promotion as a case officer.

The DAG study also identified career development as an area of improvement, noting the importance of intentional development for all officers. Indeed, one female DS&T officer who entered on duty in the mid-2010s highlighted the discrepancy between women's and men's career goals: Men have career developmental goals, whereas women, in her experience, were expected to view their careers incrementally, from job to job.[8,9] (I can't help but wonder if that's a holdover of the long-held mindset that women could get pregnant and leave at any time.) What's more, she observed men getting promoted and offered key assignments over competent, hardworking women with an unstated implication that the men were owed something, whereas the opposite was true for women, i.e., "Why should we do this for women?"

Observations like these discouraged women from being their authentic selves at work, prompting them to do things like code switch in an effort to be successful. "I think we have to do so to survive in a system that's been built for SWAMs by SWAMs," that same DS&T officer told me. She hasn't just learned to survive—she's learned to play the game doing things like personally seeking out additional SWAM mentors so that she can understand how to climb the ladder from their point of view and opting to email with her gender-neutral name and PhD in the signature block rather than pick up the secure telephone and allow them to hear her feminine voice. And while some women found support in the Agency resource groups, she noted that as a South Asian woman, she and other South Asian women avoided canoodling with each other in places like the headquarters cafeteria or Starbucks due to the stereotype that South Asian women gossip. It was decisions like these, she told me, that begin to weigh on a person. The cognitive load that she brought into every meeting as both a woman and a minority could grow tiresome.[10]

Kathleen

While Mary was taking on more influential roles at headquarters, Kathleen was gearing up for another overseas tour. Before departing, however, she spent time as the COPS in Near East Division, while Joe underwent rehabilitation for his injuries. This position turned out to be pivotal for Kathleen, setting her up for subsequent promotions due in large part to a chief who sought and gave her opportunities to excel. The deputy chief role was empty for a while, which meant more exposure to the front office for Kathleen, including plenty of briefing opportunities. Her chief took her under his wing, mentoring her on how to brief Congress and adjust the tone of her voice so that they didn't "eat her alive." He continuously pushed her forward to go to meetings in his stead, which meant that when the time came to apply for her next tour, senior leadership was familiar with her and her capabilities. As a result, Kathleen landed a tour as COPS in a prestigious European Station, and with Joe now retired, she readily accepted.

In her role as COPS in the station, she often worked closely with liaison partners, but she also made time to run her own cases. She didn't have to do this, but she believed in leading by example. She had the time, and more than that, she wanted to do it. Of course, she didn't carry a full caseload—that would have been difficult to do while overseeing all of the other operations in Station—but she carried just enough so that she could still scratch that operations itch that every case officer knows all too well.

Kathleen's management on this tour was a mixed bag. The COS was confident and didn't need any affirmation; he was one of those leaders who believed if Station looked good, then he looked good. The deputy chief, on the other hand, was a different story. She was on Kathleen's interview panel, and Kathleen was not her first choice for the COPS position. She was older than Kathleen and came from the generation that believed for a woman to get ahead she needed to take on masculine traits, and in turn, she valued those masculine traits in other people whether they were male or female. But Kathleen didn't have such attributes. She spoke softly and smiled a lot—a stark contrast from her deputy, whom she viewed as too abrupt and rude. It was clear there was a mutual dislike of each other. More than that, their optics were very different operationally.

"I don't know if I can work with this person; we're impeding each other," Kathleen told her chief.

The COS, however, was soft-spoken and appreciated his deputy's more direct approach. She was the bad cop to his good, and they worked together quite well as a management team. He valued both Kathleen's contributions and his deputy's, and so, he was between a rock and a hard place.

"You have a lot to learn from her, so try to make it work," he told Kathleen. Thankfully, neither the DCOS nor Kathleen were vindictive, and the two were able to work together professionally, although Kathleen told me that it was often awkward and unpleasant.

"She's still in [the Agency] and very senior. Prosperous," Kathleen told me. "You get the sense that the Agency values these stereotypical masculine traits . . . what I would characterize as aggressive and difficult, now we'll call that assertive and tenacious."

Kathleen went on to serve two more tours before retiring—both as chiefs of station. Similar to her previous tour as COPS, she maintained her own cases in addition to her management duties. Of course, now that she was COS, they weren't necessarily impactful cases or ones that required heavy lifting. She left those for her line operations officers. Some twenty years had passed since she began her career at the Agency and experienced intense discrimination as an Asian American first tour officer, but even as COS so many years later, Kathleen was still experiencing some of that. A senior foreign liaison officer, for example, breezed right past her at the agreed meeting location looking for a "white or Black female." Other times, if she attended a meeting with her deputy, the liaison service would assume *he* was the COS. "I'm the COS; he's the deputy," she would tell them confidently, while at the same time being extra careful that it didn't affect relations.

"I can't say it bothered me. I guess my expectations were kind of low," she told me.

What *did* bother Kathleen, however, was when her deputy went to meetings in her place and the foreign counterpart assumed *he* was in charge. "He has the responsibility to disabuse that notion, but that didn't always happen." Kathleen attributes it to male officers who may have spouses who are stay-at-home moms or gave up their careers to follow their husbands. "How they relate to women is how they see women at home. It's not necessarily to denigrate you or be contemptuous, but that's how they see women and maybe their unconscious bias or preconceived notion is being projected there." While initially offended, Kathleen decided to address it with them because as she noted, espionage is the business of dealing with people who are different from you and trying to win them over, making it all the more important to be aware of your unconscious bias and the messages you may be inadvertently sending your targets. It's wisdom and perspective like this that strike me in our conversations three years after Kathleen retired from the Agency.

A soft-spoken woman who currently spends her days learning to play piano and oil painting, you'd never guess she once led the life of a highly accomplished clandestine operative. Her life now is what some may consider quite normal—if practicing the piano for three to four hours a day until your fingers and back start hurting sounds normal to you. It seems Kathleen's same dedication to her career has carried over into her hobbies in retirement. The truth is, she doesn't know how to gauge a "normal life" and readily accepts that she may never see the world from the perspective a civilian.

"We've become desensitized or perhaps our sense of objectivity overruled . . . suppressing our normal sensory responses." But Kathleen is learning how to feel again through the wonders of music and art with her very own Indiana Jones meets James Bond still by her side.

Denise

Like Mary and Kathleen, Denise also began the 2010s at headquarters. On the heels of a successful tour as a line operations officer in the Horn of Africa, she spent the next year as a deputy chief in Africa Division, which, coincidentally, is where I met her. I had just transitioned from analytic work to clandestine operations, and I had the good fortune of working for Denise, whom I knew right away was a no-nonsense badass I could learn from. The more I learned about her story, having started her Agency career as a secretary, the more respect I had for her. You just didn't see many women in senior positions like that in the DO, and I couldn't wrap my brain around the fact that she had clawed her way there without a college degree. *How did she do it?*

What I didn't know until more than ten years later, when I interviewed Denise for this book, is that it wasn't always easy for her, although she certainly made it look that way. She had made sacrifices professionally and personally to get to where she was by the time our career paths crossed. But some of her hard times were just beginning. After serving in this deputy role for a year, Denise went to the African Sahel as a deputy chief of station. A DCOS position after having only served one tour as an operations officer is virtually unheard of and speaks to how competent, talented, and dedicated to the mission Denise was. Of course, she had already been working at the Agency for more than twenty years at this point. Denise didn't just serve as the deputy in her new station though; she was called upon almost immediately to serve as acting chief, and with that, the work pressure began to compound.

When both life and work got hard for her, Denise found herself turning to alcohol as a self-medicating tool. It's not a stretch for this to happen, given that alcohol often plays a role in meeting intelligence targets and assets, and I've already mentioned how ingrained in the CIA's culture it is. It was at this point, however, that it got out of hand for Denise. After being medically evacuated once to London, Denise decided that she needed to return to headquarters short of tour—undoubtedly a painstakingly difficult and humbling decision. She needed to make changes, and she leaned on family and the Agency's resources in order to do that while she worked a stable nine-to-five job at headquarters.

Working a less demanding job without crises felt good for Denise. It felt solid. She never lost her impeccable work ethic, but this allowed her to do the personal work she needed to do in order to get to a healthy place to return to ops in the field. She attributes this interlude of sorts to making her a better manager. "I can help employees having issues and ask the right questions," she said. (I remember her already being fantastic at this, so I can only imagine how much more this added to her chops as a manager.) After two years, Denise was ready to get back out to the field. But instead of Africa, Denise chose Latin America (LA) Division. The time zones were closer to headquarters, and it still had a bit of that "Wild West" feel she loved about Africa.

First, Denise served in an ops position at headquarters, putting in her time to become a "bankable commodity." When she learned they needed a deputy in a Latin American station, LA Division put her in Spanish-language training. They offered her eight months to learn, but she needed only five. In December 2014, she departed for a tour as DCOS in a field station in Latin America, where she often worked seventy to eighty hours a week, picking up extra cases because the office was so short-staffed. Her time at headquarters prior to this tour meant she was in a much better head space and prepared for the workload and stress.

"The role of deputy can be demanding," Denise told me. "You have all the responsibility of taking care of everyone below you, their professional development, reaching milestones, and you're then accountable to the chief. You get all the complaints, but you can't unilaterally make decisions and change things." Add to that, Denise had a demanding COS that first year. People warned her that he was tough, and yet she liked him tremendously. Her next COS was a woman, whom Denise liked even more.

"Those were some of the best years of my career. I was firing on all cylinders," she told me. Indeed, she had hit the point in her career where she felt a confluence of confidence, genuine skills, and comfort with who she was. "I would say, 'I'm not here to make friends—I have enough friends. I just want to work together and do amazing things.' Not everyone took that well," she admitted.

Nevertheless, Denise believed her main job as a manager was to be consistent and steady for junior people. And she was successful. One of the reasons for that was the tone that her new COS set for Station. This COS was far more focused on making sure people felt supported in their career and in the specific work they were doing in the office. She cared a lot about families, which Denise noted was important in the field because everything that happens at home is magnified overseas. The COS didn't just say "people should spend time with families," she modeled it by doing it herself. She kept flexible hours, made time to attend school board meetings, and didn't care what time people came in and left. When she arrived, Station felt more like a family.

After a successful three years there, Denise completed several months of training and deployed to the war zone for her next tour. Trump was president, and the South Asia Strategy kicked off. The goal was to double down—push the Taliban back and make permanent changes. It was a tremendous amount of go, go, go. Denise was a manager, and the work environment was intense. It felt like a worthy cause at the time, but when she reflected on it with me years later, she told me she wasn't so sure anymore.

"In the fog of everything happening at once, I don't know if people can really distill it and rack and stack priorities." On top of that, there were a large number of personnel problems. "The worst of people's personalities come out in an environment like that," Denise said.

Management was heavily dominated by former special forces—"war hero ground-pounder types," as she called them. "Testosterone was thick in the air. The boss would walk around and say, 'Hey, sister.' He couldn't remember my name. I sat in a morning meeting with him six days a week, but he couldn't be bothered to remember my name because I wasn't a dick-swinging ground pounder."

That didn't stop Denise from hitting the ground running. There were some hiccups in the beginning related to a female manager, whom she described as a "viper in their midst" and the embodiment of what men like to accuse women of being—backstabbing, insecure, and toxic. When this manager moved on and a new deputy arrived, the energy in the office changed. It was finally a positive place to be.

Soon after, Denise had the unfortunate fate of tripping and falling down a set of stairs in Station. She took steroids to manage the pain but stopped short of using pain medication because she was carrying a weapon. She decided to fly back to Washington for an MRI on her back, where she learned she had herniated a couple of discs in the fall. But that wasn't all the doctors saw.

"There's a shadow on your left kidney, and I don't like it. I think it might be kidney cancer," the doctor told her. Perhaps that fall wasn't so unfortunate after all.

"How fast does kidney cancer grow?" She was only three months into her one-year tour.

"It's generally pretty slow-growing."

"I only have nine months left there. Do you think it would be all right?"

"Probably, but you probably have cancer . . ."

"Let me just finish my tour up," Denise said definitively. She didn't want to pull out short of tour both because she was dedicated to the mission and for the more practical reason that she was saving to buy a house. And so, she returned to the war zone to finish out her tour, where the COS placed a plaque at the top of the staircase with her call sign.

Denise did complete her tour as planned, and when she returned to Washington, she received confirmation that the suspicious spot on her kidney was in fact cancer. That part wasn't a surprise to her. But what *was* surprising was how fast it grew.

"You waited too long. You should have come to us a year ago," the doctor told her. The cancer had spread so rapidly that Denise lost her whole kidney—one of the consequences of placing the mission above her own health.

NAME: LAURA THOMAS
YEAR OF BIRTH: 1983
PLACE OF BIRTH: PINE LEVEL, NORTH CAROLINA
ENTRANCE ON DUTY: 2009
FIELD TRADECRAFT CERTIFICATION: YES
HOME BASE: NEAR EAST DIVISION
FOREIGN LANGUAGES: ARABIC AND TWO OTHER HARD-TARGET LANGUAGES

While Mary, Kathleen, and Denise were in their final decade at the Agency as senior case officers, a new wave of female officers were beginning at Langley, including a woman named Laura Thomas, an Arabic speaker from North Carolina.

Laura was a trainee in 2010, getting her bearings at headquarters doing desk rotations before choosing a career track and heading to the Farm, having entered on duty just one year earlier. She spoke Arabic and was interested in the Middle East—she was a freshman at the University of North Carolina (UNC) on 9/11 and remembered seeing the second tower hit.

The attacks motivated her to enroll in a counterterrorism class and learn Arabic in hopes of doing her part in preventing another 9/11. "I wanted to protect Americans and work to do something to protect people in general, especially vulnerable people." She credits her family for instilling in her a sense of service to others and time studying abroad in Jordan for giving her a better understanding of the Middle East.[11]

"My view of wanting to protect America was reinforced, but after living in the Middle East and experiencing a shared humanity, it had expanded to wanting to protect so many others," she told me of her time studying in the region. She applied to the Agency shortly after graduation. Thinking she had to be a native Arabic speaker to be a case officer, she checked "analyst" on her application. But it was the DO who called first. After a lengthy hiring process, Laura started at the Agency in 2009.

She spent her first few years as a trainee, and then it was time for Laura to choose a career track. She opted for CMO because she thought it was a bit more cerebral—she loved digging into what the intelligence was saying and found it mentally stimulating. But she soon realized it wouldn't be enough for her to provide case officers with questions for their assets and review their reports; she wanted the glory of meeting with the assets and collecting her own intelligence. And so, she became a hybrid, meaning a ops-certified CMO, who, with the COS's approval, can recruit and handle assets in addition to reports duties.

For the most part, Laura felt an awareness and appreciation for the women who blazed the trail for her, but noted that even then, she had a few run-ins with the patriarchy. On her first tour, for example, when she asked her chief of base (COB) for a bottle of champagne to toast the New Year with her asset, he denied her request.

"Women can't be trusted when they drink," he told her. "In my experience, women, you don't know what you're gonna say. You might end up dancing on the table. I'll give you one beer and you can split it between you and the asset." Laura was perplexed. She hadn't done anything to make him think she was unstable. Fortunately, he was eventually removed from his position as COB—it turns out the dancing on the table comment wasn't the only questionable thing he had done. And Laura, a first-tour officer, was put in charge, in a war zone no less. It was her first exposure to leadership and gave her a better understanding of the stakes—who to bring on base, who doesn't need to be searched, etc. This was just a year after Khost, which some believed had a setback effect for women in operations and leadership positions. Laura experienced this firsthand; on more than one occasion, someone told her not to "turn into the lady at Khost." The pressure she felt on that tour was palpable.

When she returned to headquarters, Laura secured her next tour in a Middle Eastern country where she had a stellar COS, who gave her significant latitude. She handled a number of sensitive hard-target assets, and she even had recruitments, both remarkable accomplishments, especially for a CMO. She found that as a female officer, she could be a force multiplier for Station; she was highly perceptive of changing moods, motivations, and vulnerabilities. There were times, however, that she was faced with flirtatious and even aggressive advances from her sources. Without any type of training from the Agency on how to handle these types of scenarios, Laura developed her own mechanisms for dealing with them, often through some type of deflection that allowed the man to save face.

"Women begin to learn from an early age that they must find a way to deflect this behavior while also protecting men's egos," she said. She'd often redirect the conversation to family, telling the source he reminded her of her brother or father. "Usually this was enough," she said. "It was the indirect signal the man needed."[12]

By the end of her tour, Laura had created a good name for herself, and she was known as a solid officer. At the same time her career was progressing, however, Laura's marriage to a male case officer came to an end when she realized she was gay. After returning to the States, she met a woman online who two years later would become her wife. In order to PCS with Laura, her wife had to obtain a visa as her maid because the South Asian country where they were going didn't recognize gay marriage.

And so, when Laura came home from Station and saw dishes in the sink in their home in South Asia, she affectionately teased her wife that she wasn't fulfilling her "maid duties" and could be sent home short of tour. And they would laugh. Because that's all they could do.

Apart from some small logistical challenges like visas, Laura said being gay wasn't an issue for her in Station. She acknowledged that there were certainly sources she had to meet with whom she knew likely vehemently disagreed with her on a number of different topics—topics that on a personal level were quite important to her. But the work of a case officer requires empathy so that you can connect with assets, even when you and the person don't share the same values.

"It's our job to tell the truth and report the world as we see it, not as we wish it were," she told me. "When you're trying to recruit a source, it's about national security. I'm not there to change their worldview. I'm there to get information. Though sometimes changing worldviews was also a result."

She went on to say that she was cognizant of the fact that the mission was to find someone who could help our government understand foreign governments or nonstate actors in an effort to save lives. "Not just American lives. But lives," she specified.

It was this strategic view that Laura said took precedence over any personal disagreement or lack of tolerance for her on a personal level. Moreover, she felt that being gay helped her empathize with assets. "As a gay case officer, there was so much I had to hide when operating overseas and in the community where I grew up," she told me. "There are so many different parts of their lives they had to hide too. I could very much understand and empathize with that."

Still, there were tours Laura turned down due to the hostile environment for members of the LGBTQ community. When she was offered to return to a previous station in the Middle East as the deputy, she knew her wife would be pregnant during that tour, which informed her decision to decline the assignment. Laura couldn't shake the fear of something happening to one of them, like a car accident, for example, and the other not having access to them in the hospital, particularly in an end-of-life scenario. Management was willing to go to bat for her wife to get her a visa, but Laura said no. When I asked why, she told me she didn't want to be "that officer." She didn't want any favors. She'd rather just find somewhere else to go. But that proved to be even more complicated.

After serving as a COB so early in her career, Laura wanted to continue to move upward in terms of impact and responsibility. She had her eye on a COS position, but that was trickier than she hoped. She was a GS-14, which limited the locations she could serve as a COS—most places want a GS-15 or above—and she didn't want to go to a country where homosexuality was outright illegal. Even if they *were* willing to "look the other way," she feared possible retaliation against her family and/or other station officers. That left only a handful of places.

She began language training in preparation for a tour as COS in a small, sleepy European station. She wouldn't have the impact she desired, but there wasn't a pathway for anything more, given how time and grade worked at the Agency. When she began to have concerns about the environment for her wife and new baby there as well due to global political events, she pulled out of the tour and began looking for another COS job in a more open and tolerant environment of LGBTQ rights. She spoke to the head of the mission center and went in personally to apologize and explain why she was backing out.

"I think you're making the wrong decision," he told her plainly. "I personally wouldn't do this." There were a lot of things she could have said in response—their situations were wholly different—but instead, she bit her tongue. She didn't want to rock the boat; she was looking for another assignment after all. He offered to switch her with another officer, but Laura didn't want to be the officer who was given a garden-spot assignment because she was gay.

"I had a good reputation, and I didn't want that to tarnish it," she told me.

She was also mindful of how her decision could impact the careers of other gay officers. "I don't want to throw the 'gay card' because that sets gay people back."

That's when her mentor outside of the Agency advised her to leave the government so that she could continue to move upward in her career with an eye on returning to the intelligence community in the future.[13] She took her advice and resigned in early 2021.

Laura's experience as a gay woman in the DO was largely positive—her management was even willing to assist in obtaining a visa for her wife and swap her field assignment to a more LGBTQ-friendly location. This was due in large part to women like Tracey Ballard, the first openly gay CIA officer who came out in her polygraph examination in the late eighties. Laura also attributed her ability to marry and have a child while also excelling in her career to the fact that she and her wife as a gay couple essentially replicated the similar structures of heteronormative couples since Laura was working full-time and her wife stayed at home to care for their child. For Laura, the obstacle that held her back the most was the inconsistency in gay rights across the globe, which as she noted, was out of her control.

Laura's experience as a gay woman in the 2010s, however, wasn't necessarily emblematic of all gay women at the organization during this time. And while the landscape had certainly changed since Ballard first came out decades prior—it was no longer illegal to hold a top security clearance as an openly gay person—it would be inaccurate to assume that discrimination against members of the LGBTQ community had come to a screeching halt. In fact, I spoke to a different current CIA case officer, who experienced intense discrimination from a colleague, whom she described as misogynistic and homophobic, even well into her career. It got so bad, she told me, that she was brought back short of tour and had future tours blocked. While instances like this remain, the days of Agency employees having to choose between being honest about who they were or keeping their job are over.

"We are not our grandfather's organization. That's not who we are anymore," Ballard said. "There were so many that came before me that . . . served their country well, but they did so closeted. Nobody else has to go through that when they join our agency, and that's really important to me."[14]

NAME: ELYSE*
YEAR OF BIRTH: 1992
PLACE OF BIRTH: FLORIDA
ENTRANCE ON DUTY: 2015
FIELD TRADECRAFT CERTIFICATION: YES
HOME BASE: EUROPE EURASIA MISSION CENTER
FOREIGN LANGUAGES: RUSSIAN, ARABIC

Elyse moved to North Carolina with her family at age eleven, and like Laura, she always wanted to travel the world and escape the trappings of her small-town life. She too studied Arabic at UNC, along with Russian, although she and Laura didn't overlap, given their nine-year age difference. While at UNC, Elyse interned with the U.S. Department of State one summer in Latvia, which whetted her appetite for an international career. She had even started dating a communications officer at the Agency while working abroad, which she admitted also influenced her decision to work at the CIA, at least partially. She began attending information sessions whenever the CIA recruiter was on her campus and decided to apply at the start of her senior year.

"You know, you remind me a lot of myself when I was your age," the recruiter said to her. "And I just want to warn you . . . make sure you've thought about this, because the Agency is a really difficult place to work in your early twenties. I came in right out of college just like you're trying to do. All my friends were off living their lives, making mistakes. . . . There's not as much room for error at the Agency. I just want to make sure you really think about this and that it's what you want."

It seemed like odd advice at the time, particularly from someone interviewing her to work for the very organization he represented. She was there because she wanted the job. And so she blew off the recruiter's advice. Years later, she'd remember it very clearly.

"I think back to it and sometimes wonder, *What if I had followed that advice?*" she told me. Instead, Elyse went through the hiring process, which took about a year and a half.

"What's this about?" the Agency psychologist asked, referring to a recent injury to her nose Elyse listed on the paperwork. All applicants were required to meet with the psychologist, and she assumed the injury question was a way to gauge their affinity for risk.

"It's from tae kwon do," she told him, decidedly upbeat despite the negative outcome.

"Never lose that optimism," the psychologist said.

"It was almost prophetic," she told me. And then, with an unmistakable heaviness in her voice: "I lost so much of that optimism working there over the years."

Elyse graduated from UNC in August 2014 and started at the CIA in January 2015 (the very same month I resigned). Elyse likes to say that she was a "child bride to the organization," sold into marriage at a young age without knowing what she was getting into—despite the prescient warning from her recruiter.

She came on board as a professional trainee (PT), which meant she'd endure two and a half years of interim assignments before going down to the Farm for her field tradecraft certification. Before she started her interims, she went to the Farm for an initial training course. All the students would hang out in the SRB, the bar on campus, drinking together, after class each day.

One of her classmates came up to her and said, "I've been watching you. You have a nice ass."

He was a bit older than she was, a military guy in his early thirties. She was flabbergasted. The two of them had never even exchanged names, she told me. This was the first thing he said to her. A different male classmate she had been talking to told him to go away. From then on, Elyse told everyone she knew that he was a creep and to stay away from him. People would make up excuses for his "quirky sense of humor," but she got the sense that it was more than that.

At the end of the course, Elyse returned to headquarters to begin her first of four seven-month interims. She landed in the Counterterrorism Center, and when she arrived that first day, they didn't have a desk for her.

"Just hot seat in this desk while they're TDY," her new manager told her.

Elyse sat down at the desk and looked around at the photos. She noticed one in particular of a man who looked like he was sleeping. Then it dawned on her that she was at the motherfucking CIA working on counterterrorism. That guy wasn't sleeping. He was dead. *What am I getting myself into?* she thought to herself. But she ended up loving both the office and her colleagues. Her management even let her brief the current director of the CIA, John Brennan, a hell of an opportunity for a trainee, one that wasn't lost on Elyse.

"It was an incredible experience . . . so great of management to give me that opportunity," she told me.

She had three more interims after that. While some trainees are frustrated by the long runway before the Farm, Elyse enjoyed it. Every seven months, she got to experience a new office with new people and different work. At the time, she was caught up in how new and exciting all of it was. She was twenty-two years old, after all.

"I don't think I really started to notice a lot of the underlying issues until many years later," she said.

About a year into her interims, Elyse went to a trainee happy hour for people going to the Farm. She was standing in a circle of classmates talking when she felt someone's finger touch the skin of her bare back.

"You have a hole in the back of your blouse," another trainee said to her. Her long-sleeved blouse was coming apart at the seam. It was the same man from the Farm who had commented on her derriere. The comment, along with his touch, sent shivers down her spine. Several years later, he would go on to rape a friend of hers, Elyse told me.

"To this day, I wish I would have reported his behavior when we were trainees. But no one would have listened. No one would have cared," she told me. "I don't ever recall being told, 'Here's what you do if you were sexually harassed.' There was no guidance for that. I remember getting the feeling as a trainee of like, well you know, this is a tough good ole boys', man's world thing. If you're to succeed here as a woman, you are to accept it. Roll with the punches and not cause a stink." And then, as so many of us do, she explained her behavior to me, almost apologetically, "I was in my early twenties, super young and impressionable. I just kind of went along with it and didn't really question it."

I told her I understand. I was a child bride to the organization too.

Around the same time, Elyse's mom was diagnosed with brain cancer. Her friends were barhopping and living normal twentysomething professionals' lives while she was traveling about an hour every weekend to care for her dying mother. (Elyse's parents relocated from North Carolina to Virginia shortly after she began at the Agency.) Elyse was engaged to marry the communications officer she had begun dating on her State Department internship in Latvia years earlier, and her mother had been trying to survive long enough make it to the wedding. Sadly, she passed away less than three weeks before the big day, during Elyse's fourth interim assignment. Two months after her nuptials, it was finally time for Elyse to go to the Farm for her ops certification. It was a roller coaster of emotions, but she thought the distraction could be good. And in a way, it was. She was focused on something else entirely, but that also meant she didn't have time to properly process her mother's death, leading to unresolved grief later.

"My time down there wasn't fun," she told me. "Sure, there were funny moments you laugh about looking back on, but as a whole, you're running a marathon with one leg tied behind your back. Hopping along, just trying to make it through the day." The instructors created artificial stress by overwhelming trainees with assignments and artificial deadlines, and they were all just trying to stay afloat. Elyse, fortunately, had some good instructors, but she had female colleagues who regularly fielded advances from the older experienced instructors. One instructor in particular was sent down to "dry out," but was always plastered, even driving drunk on training exercises.

"There's always drama at the Farm. Thankfully, I avoided that," she told me. She had surreal moments of *I can't believe I get to do this.* But at the same time, she wondered, *Do I really want to do this for the rest of my life?*

"What was giving you pause?" I asked her.

"I don't know . . . looking back, and I think it was more of a sense of *Will this be enough to keep me engaged or happy?* But at the time, everyone is miserable when you're down there." And so, Elyse shut out any doubts she had in her mind and told herself that she wasn't the only one questioning her career choice. They were all miserable. Besides, everyone said training at the Farm was nothing like the actual job, so she decided to give it a real chance. To buckle down and get through it. For some of the trainees, it was the most stressful experience they had ever gone through, but for Elyse, having recently lost her mother, she was just thankful no one was dying. Indeed, her whole experience was colored by grief. During one operational meeting when her instructor brought up genealogy while role-playing, she shut down. Genealogy was one of her mother's favorite hobbies.

In the feedback session that followed the meeting, the instructor wanted to know what went wrong. "Are you intelligent?"

Elyse didn't know how to answer.

"Would you say that you're able to talk to people?"

Again, she wasn't sure what sort of response he was looking for, so she sat there.

"Do you have friends?" he asked. And then, finally: "What the hell happened in that meeting? You were completely closed off."

"Do you want to know the truth or do you want the professional answer?" she asked.

"The truth."

Elyse proceeded to tell him that her mom had just passed away and when he mentioned genealogy, she became overwhelmed with grief and couldn't continue the meeting productively. She began to cry as she explained this to him. That's when he pushed the feedback paperwork aside on the desk in front of him and began a series of questions: "Are you eating?" "Are you sleeping?" "Are you taking care of yourself?" What was supposed to be a thirty-minute session became a whole hour. He was checking on her as a human being. He even shared with her that he had lost his mom and couldn't imagine if he had been younger when she passed like Elyse was. She appreciated the real human connection, a stark contrast from of the other instructors who were "dicks for the sake of being dicks," she told me.

Elyse got through the Farm, and soon after, she PCSed on her husband's orders to a country in the Middle East. She was working remotely for another station, which meant she did a lot of travel. Things with her new husband, however, went downhill rather quickly. A combination of the grief over losing her mother and the fact that they never should have married in the first place, she told me. They divorced when they returned to headquarters in 2018. Soon after, she became romantically involved with another officer, a few years older than she was.

The two had been dating about five months when it went sour in December 2018, when Elyse alleges he verbally, physically, and sexually assaulted her while they were vacationing in Paris, prompting her to end the relationship.

"It was an emotionally abusive and manipulative relationship from the start," Elyse said. "He had all the power and would routinely do or say really horrible things to make me come crawling back . . . isolating me from friends and family."

She told a friend about the incident in Paris, who unbeknownst to her, reported it to security. The following week, Elyse's management called her into their office for a meeting. They said they'd tell the male officer that he couldn't go near her. And for a time after this, it seemed like it had worked. He stopped harassing and approaching her. But even then, Elyse lived in fear that she'd run into him. She'd go out of her way to walk on different floors just to avoid him.

A year later, a change in management meant a new chief/intelligence (chief/int), the person in charge of all the mission center's CMOs, including Elyse. This new chief/int didn't follow the guidelines put in place and repeatedly put Elyse in situations where she came face-to-face with the male officer. She told Elyse if she didn't feel comfortable being in the same room with him, *she* could secure video teleconference in for the meeting.

"Look, I don't know if you know the definition of sexual assault, but this is unacceptable," Elyse told her.

Her manager backed down.

"The fact that I had to advocate for myself as a victim . . . and to a woman . . . a female leader, no less, is super fucked up," she told me. "I do think there is a culture within the Agency among female senior leadership. This mindset of 'I had to deal with it, you should just suck it up and deal.'"

Despite these difficulties, Elyse loved her job working Eastern European issues on a team that valued her skill set. Even so, she felt deep in her gut that something wasn't right about the way the Paris incident was handled.[15]

Meanwhile, the DAG study was complete with a long list of deliverables, including an on-ramping/off-ramping toolkit, analysis of enterprise professional development tools, a series of DAG-sponsored learning events, and a pilot telework program, among many others. Arguably a better indicator of progress, however, was in 2018 when Gina Haspel was appointed as the CIA's first female director. Her appointment meant that many women saw a new path for themselves at the Agency for the first time—one that could potentially include a leadership position at the senior-most levels of the organization.

What's more, one current female officer, while reflecting on Haspel's appointment years later, told me that she thought it highlighted the value the CIA placed on women at the organization and put CIA female officers front and center to the world. "I think it scares the living daylights out of our adversaries because there's a woman running this place, and we get it done," she said.[16] This milestone didn't come without controversy though, as many Democrats, and some Republicans, opposed Haspel's confirmation due to her role in the Agency's enhanced interrogation tactics after 9/11.[17]

Later that same year, Haspel appointed the lead implementer of the DAG study, Sonya Holt, as the Agency's chief diversity and inclusion officer. "To succeed against intelligence challenges facing us today, we must have officers who bring a variety of life experiences and viewpoints to the job," Haspel said. Months later, she named Elizabeth Kimber to the role of deputy director of CIA for operations (DDO)—the first woman to hold the position.[18] All three women each brought with them more than thirty years of experience at the Agency to their new roles, and women now made up 36 percent of the Senior Intelligence Service (SIS).[19] While it's far more likely that your average educated American will recognize Haspel's name as the first female director, Kimber's position as the director of operations was arguably a more important milestone for women. Indeed, it wasn't that long ago that women were fighting to prove their ability to run operational cases, and now, a woman was overseeing the entirety of CIA's clandestine operations worldwide.

By the end of the 2010s, Denise had bounced back from kidney cancer and began a tour as COPS in a large and complex undisclosed field station, which is where she would be posted when the world shut down at the start of the next decade. Elyse would soon find herself isolated on the other side of the world, thrown into her grief and trauma, and forced to find her way out, with or without the Agency.[20]

CHAPTER 7

2020 AND BEYOND

Women were poised for more progress when the COVID-19 pandemic began in 2020, setting off the "Great Resignation," in which roughly one million women would leave the US workforce due in large part to their bearing the brunt of childcare responsibilities when schools and daycares closed and offices went remote. The impact no doubt shone a light on women's valuable roles in society, the economy, and the professional workplace, including the CIA. At the same time, women like Lewinsky and Spears were taking back control of their narratives; in 2021, Lewinsky was a producer on FX's *Impeachment: American Crime Story*, which sought to reframe the events leading up to the impeachment of President Bill Clinton.[1] And Spears broke free of a thirteen-year conservatorship that controlled her personal and business decisions. Two years later, she released a memoir, *The Woman in Me*, telling her story in her own words for the first time. It sold 1.1 million copies in the US in the first week alone.[2,3]

Even the Bond franchise was placing women at the center. In its latest installment, *No Time to Die*, released at the box office in 2021, the strong female portrayals prompted discussions about the possibility of a female James Bond—an interesting notion, given that for the first time in the CIA's history all its director-ates were led by women. Indeed, it seemed the Agency was entering a new era.

This new era, however, didn't come without its challenges. In addition to the pandemic, the start of this decade also meant the arrival of the #MeToo movement at the CIA. When news broke that CIA case officer Brian Jeffrey Raymond was arrested in 2020 and charged with videotaping a woman who was par-tially naked and unconscious, people started taking notice of sexual assault at the Agency, both within and outside of the organization. (As Lizzo would say, it's about damn time.) Prose-cutors called Raymond an "experienced sexual predator," whom the State Department and FBI began investigating after police in Mexico City responded to a report of a "naked, hysterical woman desperately screaming for help" from Raymond's bal-cony back in May 2020. The Agency would find that this inci-dent was just the tip of the iceberg. In late 2023, Raymond pled guilty for drugging and sexually assaulting more than two dozen women over a fourteen-year period while serving as a CIA case officer, and in September 2024, he was sentenced to thirty years in prison.[4] This case marked the beginning of a string of nega-tive press coverage around sexual assault cases and their alleged mishandling at the organization.

As for Mary and Denise, they were each entering their final days at the Agency. Mary had come a long way since her first assignment as an operations officer in Near East Division back in the nineties. She was using her experience as a senior female case officer to play an integral role in diversity and inclusion at the Agency and helped spearhead a study that reflected on the previous twenty years, at times wondering if anything had changed at all.[5] In 2021, she left the organization and began pur-suing other passions like health and wellness. When I met her, she was working on her fitness instructor certification. Now she finds joy teaching fitness classes regularly, and I can't help but wonder if those attending have any idea that they're learning from a former clandestine operative.

Similarly, Denise was ready for a change. As someone who had always put the organization before her personal life since joining the CIA at age nineteen, she was ready to shake things up.

Denise

When the COVID-19 pandemic first began, there was almost nothing for Denise and other officers to do at her field station, where she was serving as COPS, and everywhere else CIA was operating in the world. Think about it—when your bread and butter consists of meeting people to collect foreign intelligence, how do you do your job when people are told to stay home and not interact with each other? Officers weren't allowed to meet with their assets let alone go out and recruit new ones. There was a mad scramble to communicate with assets they wouldn't see for a while to tell them to keep the channels open and they'd be back in touch. They wanted to give them more details, more specifics, but they didn't have any answers. No one did. They kept in close contact with each other and their FBI colleagues and worked on alternating schedules. And like much of the country—and world—they passed the time by sharing pictures of their sourdough starters. Denise, for her part, taught herself how to sew masks and put them in the mail to colleagues.

When news came out that COVID could cause internal organ damage, Denise called her primary care physician for guidance.

"What are you doing going into an office? You don't have a kidney," he admonished her.

Denise stayed home for eight weeks after that. Eight weeks was all she could manage. She was clawing at the walls. She scheduled a telemedicine appointment to ask her doctor if she could go back to work.

"Wear your mask every second. Don't use public toilets. Keep your office door closed," she recalled him telling her. And then, with a doctor's note in hand, Denise returned to Station. By June, she was back full-time. She was initially "Team Gold," coming in every other week, but she would sneak back in the office on her off weeks too. She was nothing if not dedicated to the mission. But around this time, Denise decided she was ready for something more than the mission. She was ready to date. And so, she joined Bumble. If you had to choose a dating app, one that championed a woman-centered approach seemed like the best choice to her. She dated one dud for about six months, and then she changed her approach. She would use her case officer skills, she decided. And she would be choosy. She defined what she wanted and decided she wouldn't consider anyone who didn't meet those standards.

"As women, we're taught to be too polite. I just wasn't gonna do it anymore. Being too polite leads to unhappiness and settling, and I wasn't going to settle," Denise told me. She narrowed her search from the one hundred men who swiped on her down to about twenty and then eight. Then she invited them for coffee or lunch. Like a true operations officer, she could learn a lot from meeting someone in person, much more so than over text. And she didn't want to spend time texting someone if they weren't worth her time in the end. She set up her dates with her final eight men, always meeting in public and sharing a screenshot of the photo with her girlfriends. "If I don't come back, this is who killed me," she told them. But she was also confident in her ability to assess people; she was a trained CIA operative, after all.

A man named Patrick was her favorite. She enjoyed their conversation, and he was by far the funniest. She appreciated that his photos on Bumble were less polished, which communicated to her that he wasn't someone who took himself too seriously. It spoke to his boldness and confidence. After their date, like any good case officer, Denise wanted to secure that second meeting. So she looked at him and said, "If you ask me out again, I'll say yes." He gave her a long hug goodbye, and by the time she got back to her car, she received a text from him that said: "I think I just had an amazing time, and I'd like to go out on another date with you." Denise invited him over for dinner, and things progressed from there.

When she entered the final months of her tour, Denise received notification that she was selected for a COS position overseas in a French-speaking country that she had applied for in the spring, prior to meeting Patrick. What's more, the current COS was leaving early, and they wanted her to go out right away. She was only two months into her budding relationship. And for the first time, Denise chose her personal life over the mission.

She sent an email to the selection panel declining the position for personal reasons. She knew it was unexpected, but she felt good knowing that she gave them nine months lead time and a formal, official notification. Then she wrote a more personal email to the woman who was the head of the selection panel that read, "For the first time in my life, I met a nice boy, and I am not going to throw this away. I'm fifty years old. Who would have thought? I can't leave. He can't go overseas because of his job, so I'm going to step back and I'm gonna make different decisions about my life. I want you to know how important that job was to me and what it meant to even be selected." Denise admitted to me that she still chokes up about having given up an opportunity to serve as COS, as it's undoubtedly such an important milestone for any operations officer.

And in a beautiful display of women helping women, the woman wrote her back and said, "I'm so proud of you for making a decision that's based on your life and not your work. I am a mom. I have a family, and I haven't always made those decisions. And in hindsight, I sometimes wish I had done things differently. I'm really proud of you for doing that, and it can't have been easy. Whatever happens next for you, wherever you want to go, where I am, you have a job with me. You just reach out."

Denise spent another two-plus years at the Agency, choosing her positions based on her new life with Patrick, before retiring in January 2022. Not checking the COS box still stings for her as something left undone, and she sometimes wonders, *Could I have made SIS?*

A chief once told her, "There's no doubt in my mind that you'll make SIS one day. You have the drive and what it takes. Keep in mind, not everyone is going to work at your pace. What you think is eighty percent is someone else's 150 percent." It was good advice at the time and gratifying to her that someone thought she was worthy of making it into senior ranks. But even that, she told me, was "fleeting" and a bit of an "ego stroke."

"What I have at home is hopefully going to last me thirty, forty years if we can keep each other alive. What does a couple years of walking around, excuse my French, with my dick outside of my pants do? I'm not an ego tripper."

Denise remains an avid supporter of the CIA, despite having experienced her fair share of discrimination, sexual harassment, and even sexual assault there (remember the man who repeatedly grabbed her breasts in the hallway?). She reflects on her career with the wisdom and perspective of a woman who has fought her way to the top, despite some very real obstacles that were placed in her path, both personally and professionally.

"Could I have made different choices?" She poses the question when explaining that she never intended to become fifty years old, single, and without kids. "It just kinda snuck up on me," she tells me. "Nobody walks out of here without regrets, but I feel like I've gotten so much more than I've given. And I've given a lot."

Denise and Patrick are still together, and they split their time between the Washington, DC, area and Colorado, where Denise is learning to ski for the first time.

Elyse

In mid-2020, when Denise was exchanging sourdough starter tips and making masks for her colleagues, Elyse began her tour in Western Europe. She was one of the first officers to deploy after a temporary pause in PCS assignments due to the COVID pandemic. It seemed everything was falling into place for her first field tour on her own orders, and she'd finally get the quintessential field experience she had looked forward to during her grueling training at the Farm. But things didn't go as planned. A month into her tour, everything shut down again, and Elyse was alone, apart from her two cats.

Life overseas wasn't at all what it was cracked up to be. While other officers were at home with their families, Elyse felt increasingly isolated and depressed. The isolation also meant Elyse couldn't run from experiences she had bottled up and distracted herself from over the previous two years. Far from the carrot they dangled while undergoing the demanding operational training at the Farm, Elyse found it miserable.

What's more, her female COS and DCOS were decidedly unsupportive when she explained how isolated she felt without family in-country. She tried to get approval for her father to come stay with her for a few weeks, telling her management she was an only child and her mother had just passed. "None of our parents can come; we're in the same boat," was the response she received. There was simply no appetite to do anything to support single officers, Elyse told me.

By springtime the following year, Elyse and a friend of hers in a different European station wrote an article together for an inner Agency forum about the plight of being single during COVID in the field. Elyse's chief and deputy chief, both women, saw the article and were irate that Elyse didn't consult them before publishing it, she recalled to me.

The COS called her into her office and laid into her. "No one likes it when someone complains about their situation and doesn't try to fix it. What have you done to try to fix it?" the COS demanded to know before she went through each recommendation Elyse and her friend made in the article and ripped them apart line by line.

Elyse began to cry.

Days later, the deputy called Elyse in her office when the chief was out and talked about women supporting other women. Elyse was understandably confused; everything her deputy had done thus far suggested otherwise. And that's when the seeds of doubt began.

Perhaps this wasn't the career for her after all.

Elyse considered returning to Washington short of tour but decided to stick with it. From an operational standpoint, she loved the work. She was an operationally-certified CMO, having graduated from the Farm, which meant she could recruit and handle assets. She enjoyed this, although she acknowledged doing case officer work as a woman came with its own unique set of challenges.

During her very first operational meeting, the recruited asset commented on her age and looks right off the bat. "I didn't expect someone so young and pretty as you." She told him it was very kind and promptly redirected the conversation.

One of the ways she managed these types of situations was by dressing as asexual as possible. She wore pants and turtlenecks, showing minimal skin, light makeup, and very little jewelry. She also dressed for comfort, given that she often had to walk for extended periods conducting surveillance detection routes on the way to operational meetings.

"It's a strange dichotomy because being a woman can be helpful in those situations because men can sometimes reveal more to women who are young and pretty," she told me. "It's a unique balance of utilizing femininity, but you don't want things to go in the wrong direction."

If Elyse was meeting an asset in a hotel room, for example, she'd always make sure the door to the bed was closed off and not in the asset's line of vision. It wasn't lost on her that these were all things her male colleagues simply didn't have to consider for their operational meetings.[6]

Elyse managed these dynamics well and found operational successes during her first field tour. These successes, however, brought with them high levels of anxiety, to the point that she would lay awake at night before an ops meeting running through all the things that could go wrong. And after a meeting, she'd spend that night replaying it in her mind, second-guessing her decisions. To a certain extent, she considered some amount of self-doubt and anxiety as normal, perhaps even good, in this line of work. But she was beginning to think the weight of it all was becoming more than she could bear.

About halfway through Elyse's tour in Western Europe, she was sent to a liaison training course for Russian in another country. She was one of the first women to go through the training, which she told me was likely due to the fact that the Agency had a lot more male Russian speakers than female. Elyse had done operational work speaking in Russian before, but this was an opportunity to practice in a variety of scenarios, including role-playing. It was a full-immersion experience. At one point, Elyse found herself in a philosophical debate on the ethics of espionage.

"But it's treason," the foreign liaison course instructor, role-playing as a Russian target, said to her.

"Well, what *is* treason?" Elyse countered in Russian. "If treason is something that hurts your country, and this could help your country, then is that really treason?"

The two of them went back and forth, and when she received feedback after the exercise, the instructor said, "I had no idea Americans could speak Russian that well. I was very impressed by how well you handled that." Elyse appreciated the compliment and knew what high praise that was coming from a foreign liaison service.

The course was going well until they reached a new training exercise and things took a turn. The students were required to go to a bar and bump a target, which essentially meant they had to strike up a conversation with a fictitious intelligence target and secure a second meeting. The catch? They had to conduct the bump in Russian. Each CIA student was partnered with a student from the foreign liaison service. Elyse and her partner's target was an older man in his seventies who was a witting role-player, but he brought several of his drunk unwitting friends into the bar with him.

While her partner and the target were outside having a smoke, Elyse sat next to one of the unwitting, intoxicated men when he suddenly grabbed her by the top of her hair and shoved her face into his lap. She started screaming and punching him in the ribs, but he had a tight grip on her hair. Later, she'd find her scalp was bruised. Some friends from the training course saw what was happening and came over to stop it. Apparently, the man thought she was a prostitute. When her partner came back in, he called the instructors and told them to come pick them up. The instructors were all horrified, with the exception of one, who said, "Well, these sorts of things happen in real life." The others were apologetic and offered to send her back to her station early, but she opted to stay in-country and finish the course. Afterward, there wasn't any mention of what happened to her—no offer for psychological support or anything of the sort.

"It was just swept under the rug," Elyse told me. "'We just don't talk about it' was very much the mindset."

She remembers the predominant feeling she had afterward: rage. It was yet another reminder that at the end of the day, spying was still very much a man's world. Months before her tour ended, the Agency set up a new office for dealing with sexual assault called the Sexual Assault Prevention Office (SAPRO). The office was the result of grassroots efforts by an internal organization called Sexual Assault Survivors. (On a visit to CIA headquarters in 2023, I was shocked to see how out in the open the office was—in a major thoroughfare with a sign on the outside of the door: "Sexual Assault Prevention Office." I couldn't help but wonder, *What victim would feel comfortable walking into an office with a sign plastered on the outside announcing it's where you go to report sexual assault?* For an organization grounded in secrecy, it sure didn't feel discreet.)

When Elyse saw an email about SAPRO, she reached out to the woman in charge and asked if she'd be willing to hear her story. The woman said yes, and the next day the two of them had a phone call on the secure line. Elyse told her no one had ever reached back out to her with closure after she reported her assault. Her friends kept an eye on cable traffic to make sure he was far away from her, but no one from security had contacted Elyse to tell her what actions were taken. She wanted to know, *What happened to him? What, if anything, did the Agency do?* The next day the woman reached out to inform her that he had been separated from the Agency and his clearances were revoked.

"I know it took four years, but your voice was finally heard," the woman told her.[7]

Back at headquarters, Elyse began the process of getting her résumé cleared so she could look for jobs outside of the Agency. She was miserable each time she walked into the building, constantly reminded of the trauma she experienced prior to her tour in Europe. Moreover, she had spent her home leave on the heels of her tour with a college friend and her husband in North Carolina, which gave her a peek into what life on the outside could be like. She looked at their life together, working in the private sector and traveling internationally three to four times a year, and thought, *I want* this *life*. It was a stark contrast to how she felt when she looked at the lives of her senior female managers at the CIA, many of whom either didn't marry or were divorced.

As Elyse was interviewing for jobs outside of the Agency, she came across an article written by two female officers on one of the CIA's internal blogs—a call to action that shared publicly within the Agency one of their own experiences and asked other victims of sexual harassment and sexual assault to submit victim impact statements to be shared with the seventh floor. Elyse reached out to the officers listed on the article, and they put her in touch with another sexual assault survivor at the Agency. The two of them swapped stories, and for the first time, Elyse saw what happened to her through someone else's eyes. She felt the weight of what she had endured.

"It's easier to have compassion for someone else other than yourself," she told me. "That was the moment where I realized that this wasn't handled well or appropriately." Elyse learned that thanks to one of those brave female officers who shared her sexual assault incident on the internal blog, Congress's House Permanent Select Committee on Intelligence (HPSCI) had begun an investigation of the CIA's handling of sexual harassment and sexual assault cases. Soon after, the Senate Select Committee on Intelligence Committee (SSCI) called on the CIA inspector general to initiate an immediate investigation.

Having already made up her mind to resign from the Agency, Elyse decided she wanted to do what she could to help before she left. With support and guidance from the other women, Elyse first met with the HPSCI and then the Office of the Inspector General (OGI), and last, the SSCI. After each meeting, she was emotionally drained, having to relive the experiences over and over. At the same time, she found that talking about it brought some relief, as if a weight was lifted after all these years. Elyse told Congress that she felt comfortable speaking to them only because she was leaving the organization and that these experiences were a large part of her decision to resign. She wondered how many women were too afraid to speak up because they were still working at the Agency and feared retribution.

In response to the HPSCI's investigation, the Agency issued a press release on the steps it was taking to handle allegations of sexual assault and harassment, which included the appointment of Dr. Taleeta Jackson, a psychologist who oversaw the US Navy's sexual assault prevention program, to lead the CIA's office dedicated to handling these incidents, Sexual Assault Prevention Office (SAPRO)—the same office Elyse had reached out to a year earlier to find out what became of her report.[8] (SAPRO was previously led by a former finance officer from the Directorate of Support (DS). In late 2023, the office was renamed the Sexual Harassment/Assault Response and Prevention Office (SHARP).)

While sexual harassment and sexual assault at the CIA has prompted press releases from Langley—several other cases have gained the media's attention over the past two years—women in senior leadership have largely been quiet on the issue. "There's a culture of fear that surrounds the topic of sexual harassment and assault, and that's a huge part of the reason why it's been allowed to propagate for so long," Elyse told me.

"The majority of women at the senior levels don't feel like they are able to stick their neck out for other women without facing repercussions themselves." She believes this is a large reason why this behavior has gone unchecked for so long. "A lot of senior women have been complicit and looked the other way, instead of standing shoulder to shoulder and saying, 'We're not going to allow this.'"

Elyse, however, acknowledged the need for women at the CIA, noting that there were so many things she was able to do operationally *because* she's a woman. "It really is an advantage in this line of work, being underestimated." And while staying at the Agency felt untenable for her, she's hopeful that other women's experiences moving forward will be different. "The reason I'm talking to you is because I don't want future generations of young women to have the experience I've had here," she recalled telling Congress. "I want this place to be better for other women."[9]

While women like Kathleen, Mary, and Denise were closing their chapters at the CIA at the start of this decade, 2020 ignited a reckoning of sorts at the Agency that meant a different environment for the women who remained—an environment in which women have begun to speak out against inequities, harassment, and assault. An environment where women were much more likely to help other women, whether that was recommending them for a position, pitching in when they needed extra assistance due to family commitments, or banding together to create a better environment for future generations of women.

Women at the Agency, especially case officers, operate in an environment where men have long held the power, but the tides are finally turning. "It's a new generation," one current senior female case officer told me. In December 2023, Congress passed the Intelligence Authorization Act, requiring the CIA to establish and implement reporting mechanisms for sexual harassment and sexual assault that include congressional oversight—an important step toward accountability in a culture of secrecy and male dominance that has kept women from coming forward for decades. The act is part of the National Defense Authorization Act for Fiscal Year 2024 and is a direct result of the dozens of women, including Elyse, who, since January 2023, have shared their stories with Congress.

EPILOGUE

"How do you do it? How does one have it all?" one junior CIA officer asked her female mentor.

"Oh, you don't. Ever," the senior officer answered. "One time you'll be on an operation and leave your kid at home with a fever and maybe not see them. That's just part of it. Or you'll be at home with your kid with a fever and miss the operation. You'll always do one thing good, and okay at the other."

This pressure to "have it all" isn't unique to espionage. Women have felt the pressure to "lean in" since Sheryl Sandberg first coined the term in her book *Lean In: Women, Work, and the Will to Lead* published in 2013. In the past decade, however, women have begun to push back against this concept. Michelle Obama spoke candidly about it on her 2018 book tour for her memoir, *Becoming*, saying, "I tell women that whole 'so you can have it all' . . . That's a lie. And it's not always enough to lean in, because that shit doesn't work all the time."[1]

My conversations with women during a visit to headquarters in 2023 echoed this sentiment. One officer told me that she didn't believe anyone's life was truly balanced and that she disliked the term "work-life balance."

"It's a societally imposed goal," she said. "You're supposed to strive to balance the roles in your life to the detriment of your work, your family, and your friends. That you're never enough or doing it right unless you're balanced. It's not true. Technically life isn't balanced, right? It's only balanced in the moment, and life is moment to moment."

On that same visit, I was encouraged by the caliber of women who continue to be a part of the workforce. Meeting these intelligent, talented women, who aspire to be leaders at the Agency one day, underscored for me how important it is that the organization foster a healthy, safe environment for women and minorities. Indeed, it's in the CIA's best interest lest it lose competent female officers who bring unique perspectives to all aspects of Agency work and are a vital part of the mission.

Countless women I interviewed told me that there were things women just did better when it came to clandestine operations—details women noticed more than men or the fact that women could exist in the background and go completely unnoticed, like Marti, who used Russia's misogynistic world-view against itself to conduct her operations surveillance-free for months. Indeed, women are stellar officers, whether they're case officers meeting clandestine assets in the field or serving in another directorate as an analyst, technical officer, support officer, you name it.

In further conversations with female officers at headquarters, the attitude was one of progress—at least in some directorates. Women currently make up nearly half of the organization, and many have had largely positive experiences.

"Traditional gender roles are slowly being chipped away at," one female officer told me. "And some women are taking the time and space to say, 'I want this. Let's talk about how we can both advance our careers, our hobbies, and our life goals.'" The women credited much of the Agency's progress to its resource groups that highlight the critical part diversity plays in mission success.

"I really feel like that message is taking hold at the highest levels here, and it has been for quite some time. It's almost night and day from when I started as an intern," Kate, an analyst with a disability who began at the Agency in 2012, told me. What's more, Kate said that she's never questioned her ability to succeed in the DA either because she's a woman or disabled.

"I do want to be a leader in the DA here," she told me. "Just making the building better for the next person to come, particularly the next girl in a wheelchair who's also going to fall in love with this place." Of note, the CIA was selected as the Government Employer of Choice for *CAREERS & the disABLED Magazine* for 2021 and 2022, a distinction the Agency is very proud of, the chief of the public engagement group within the Office of Public Affairs told me. (Becoming an "Employer of Choice" was included in the Diversity in Leadership Study commissioned by then-director John Brennan in 2013 to determine barriers to advancement for CIA officers with disabilities.)

A DS&T officer acknowledged that while there have been some improvements, barriers for women's entry into the DS&T and leadership roles remain. "We see women at the top. We had a female director," she said. "And then, at that point, we were all really excited. But as you started going down levels, you saw it was all male, all male again, all male again." She also shared that being a mother is more of an obstacle than being a woman, as it limits her ability to work demanding hours and apply for certain positions, much like women experience outside of the organization.

One area that *has* improved is the support for new mothers; in 2020, the Agency created lactation rooms that include private stalls, refrigerators, cleaning stations, and charging cords, and on October 1, 2020, the new paid parental leave for federal employees took effect. There's even a program to support nursing mothers who are on travel. Much of the positive changes, however, have come from within the organization, driven by women themselves. The lactation rooms, for example, were a result of grassroots efforts. And while there hasn't always been an overwhelming number of women supporting women, in recent years that's changed too. In front offices that are mostly female, the women tend to look out for each other.

"They all kind of support each other and help each other through leadership and through management and learning . . . if two of them are women and then you have EAs that are also heavily female . . . step in for each other, especially when it comes to family stuff," one female officer at headquarters told me. The women at headquarters also talked about the female managers who exemplify behavior and how important that was. When one female manager boldly announces that she plans to leave at a certain time to pick up her child from daycare, it humanizes her and creates an environment where junior female officers feel more comfortable to make appropriate choices for their own personal lives.

While the CIA has improved in some areas like accessibility and parental leave, the organization continues to lack diversity—minority women only account for 13 percent of the total workforce, suggesting there is plenty of work that remains to be done. In meetings with the CIA's Talent Acquisition Office at CIA headquarters, I learned about the Agency's commitment to diversity outreach throughout the entire recruitment process, from maintaining long-standing relationships with minority serving institutions to developing corporate sponsorships with professional organizations that foster professional and academic development of underrepresented communities, including the Thurgood Marshall College Fund, Society of Asian Scientists and Engineers, and the Hispanic Association of Colleges and Universities.

However, there remains a vast disconnect between the percentage of minority women who apply to the Agency and that of actual employed minority women. For example, in fiscal year

2023, approximately half of all female applicants self-identified as minorities, and out of those applicants, approximately 35 percent of female DO applicants self-identified as minorities. And yet the current percentage of women in the DO is 41 percent, and minority women represent a mere 8 percent of the DO population. For comparison, the current percentage of women in the Directorate of Support (DS) is 55 percent, and minority women represent 22 percent of the DS population.

"If you look at data on non-retirement and departures, it starts to become obvious that we have a problem with women and minorities who are leaving early," Sue Gordon, former principal deputy director of national intelligence and CIA veteran of more than thirty years, told me.[2] "We just can't afford to be losing talent. We want to be an organization where every talented person wants to come and any talented person who can perform will succeed."[3] (The CIA was unwilling to share details with me on its retention rates and/or its efforts to retain minority women.)

CIA leadership hasn't always been aligned in this view though. In fact, two CIA case officers told me that at an internal town hall in 2022, when asked about retention rates, the CIA's deputy director for operations said that officers who left were people the Agency didn't want anyway, alleging that they either couldn't cut it or simply wanted more money in the private sector. His refusal to acknowledge issues with retention rates demonstrates a lack of accountability at the highest levels of the CIA.

"There's this overarching smugness about our specialness," Gordon told me.[4] "This is such a clear leadership moment, and the Agency continues to fail on this."

When it comes to senior leadership roles, the historic drop-off for women after GS-15 has improved in recent years. The Director's Diversity in Leadership Study published in 2015 noted the dearth of diversity at the Agency, saying that "the more senior the Agency's workforce is, the less diverse it is."[5] Since then, however, the CIA has made notable headway when it comes to women in senior roles across the Agency, including women of color. As of 2024, women accounted for a surprising 40.6 percent of SIS officers, and of the population of female SIS officers, 4.3 percent were Asian, 10.1 percent were Black or African American, 4 percent were Hispanic or Latino, 0.3 percent were American Indian or Alaskan Native, and 1.3 percent identified as two or more races. These numbers, however, do not reflect the DO, where women of color in senior leadership roles are a rarity. Multiple officers I interviewed could not think of a single Black female case officer with whom I could speak, and some even told me that there has only been one Black female operations officer who has reached the SIS level.[6]

There is, however, a risk of what two CIA officers called "DEIA fatigue."

"I think we had such a heavy shift with the executive order on DEIA and all the women in the workplace reports from McKinsey, there was a heavy push for minorities," Kate told me. "And then you have this resistance."

That hasn't stopped her from trying to effect change when it comes to accessibility at the Agency, telling me, "I am so proud of having been able to be a part of a lot of these efforts to really bring the Agency forward on this with the caveat that I can think of many things that we still need to do."

After our conversations, the head of the CIA's museum walked me through the exhibits, pointing out those that highlighted women. Of course, there was one exhibit dedicated to Virginia Hall with some artifacts—the CIA never misses an opportunity to reference "the Limping Lady," although the nickname admittedly hasn't aged well—and another display of photos of a handful of other women from the OSS with vignettes written about their accomplishments, including Hedy Johnson,

Ruth Sherman Tolman, Cora Du Bois, among others. There was also a display on Elizabeth Sudmeier, an early reports officer who functioned as an operations officer in NE division, with a "Challenging Culture" marker next to it. Selected as one of the Agency's dedicated "CIA Trailblazers" in 2013, Sudmeier earned the Intelligence Medal of Merit, controversial at the time due to her being both a woman and a reports officer.[7]

While I appreciated the effort to showcase women, I couldn't help but think it felt a bit like a box-checking exercise. Notably missing from the museum were the women responsible for watershed moments when it came to breaking down gender barriers at the CIA, like Janine and Margery. But then again, organizations tend to shy away from moments in their history that make them appear less than favorable, and the CIA is no exception. Perhaps one day, the Agency will embrace these women in addition to sexual assault survivors like Elyse, who have bravely shared their experiences with Congress, and proudly highlight their roles in the fight for women's rights at the CIA. It's my hope that the women who come after will know their names and know that because of them, the Agency is a better place for women.

What I've aimed to accomplish with this book is shed light on the remarkable women who make up the CIA, and who, like women everywhere, have made choices that have determined the path of their careers and by extension, their lives. Whether it was Kathleen waiting until her husband's retirement to take the lead, Mary Beth choosing a successful career over marriage and kids, or Denise finally choosing her romantic life over the mission when she reached her fifties, women are often faced with choices in their careers—choices that are markedly different from those of their male counterparts. Regardless of the path they chose, their contributions to intelligence were valuable and important, whether they stayed at the organization for one year or thirty.

As the CIA moves forward, it's my hope that it will build on the progress it has made when it comes to the role of women and, most important, that the Agency will continue to work to curb the systemic sexual harassment and sexual assault that has thrived in its culture of secrecy and male dominance. We need women at the CIA—without them, our national security is weaker.

So here's to the troublemakers. The trailblazers. The agents of change. May we celebrate them. May we remember them. May we be them.

GLOSSARY

ADDO: assistant deputy director of operations

CIC: Counterintelligence Center

CMO: collection management officer, also referred to as a reports officer

COB: chief of base

COPS: chief of operations

COS: chief of station

CRS: Central Reference Service

CT: career trainee

CTC: Counterterrorism Center

DA: Directorate of Analysis, previously called the Directorate of Intelligence (DI)

DAG: Director's Advisory Group

DCOS: deputy chief of station

DDO: deputy director of the CIA for operations, colloquially referred to as the "director of operations"

DI: Directorate of Intelligence, now called the Directorate of Analysis (DA)

DO: Directorate of Operations

DOWAC: Directorate of Operations Women's Advisory Council

DS: Directorate of Support

DS&T: Directorate of Science and Technology

EA: East Asia Division within the Directorate of Operations

EA: executive assistant, a prestigious role and opportunity at the CIA that is reserved for a select few senior officers

EOD: entrance on duty

EUR: Europe, used when referring to Europe Division in the Directorate of Operations

EXDIR: executive director, the CIA director's chief operating officer

FSN: foreign service national, a local citizen working at a US Embassy

FTC: field tradecraft certification

GS: general schedule, although colloquially referred to as "grade step"

HPSCI: The House Permanent Select Committee on Intelligence

IG: inspector general

JOT: Junior Officer Training

LA: Latin America Division within the Directorate of Operations

NE: Near East Division within the Directorate of Operations

NSC: National Security Council

Ops: operations, referring to clandestine operations

OSS: Office of Strategic Services

PAR: performance appraisal review

PCS: permanent change of station

PT: professional trainee

RUMINT: rumor intelligence

SAPRO: Sexual Assault Prevention Office

SCI/TK: sensitive compartment information/talent keyhole

SHARP: Sexual Harassment/Assault Response and Prevention Office

SIS: Senior Intelligence Service

SOO: staff operations officer, also referred to as a desk officer

SSCI: Senate Select Committee on Intelligence Committee

SWAM: straight, white, able, and male

TDY: temporary duty assignment

ACKNOWLEDGMENTS

Thank you to the brilliant women of the CIA, especially those of you who graciously shared your stories with me. One of the greatest joys of writing this book has been getting to know all of you. A shared experience like working at the CIA as a woman has the power to reach across generations and bond us, and for that, I'll be eternally grateful. I'm honored to tell your stories, and I hope with every fiber of my being that I've done you proud.

A very special thanks to Valerie Plame for writing the foreword and for believing in this project. I'm still pinching myself that I get to call you friend.

Thank you to Colin Thompson for our hours of discussions and emails over the past few years—what an incredible resource you've been for me! When I learned Janine passed just before I began my research, I was devastated that I wouldn't have a chance to interview or get to know her. With the help of Colin and many of her family, friends, and colleagues, including Steven Brookner, Gary Okun, Art Katcher, George Amato, and Susan Amato, I was able to tell her story. It's been an honor to portray such an important trailblazer for women at the CIA. I hope I've done her justice in your eyes.

Thank you to the CIA's PCRB for their prompt review of my manuscript. Special thanks to the CIA's Office of Public Affairs for welcoming me back to headquarters to interview current women and, of course, load up on CIA swag from the gift shop. My goal has been to write a balanced book that celebrates female CIA officers and the progress the organization has made through the decades, while not shying away from some of the more difficult times. I hope you'll be pleased with the result.

Thank you to my literary agent, Alyssa Maltese, who shared my view that the stories of these courageous women are worthy of being told even when others didn't. There were days when I thought I was crazy for choosing to return to the querying trenches, but I thank my lucky stars that I did because I found you. Thank you for welcoming me into the Root Literary family and always having my back.

Thank you to my editor, James Abbate, for your full faith in me as a writer and for fiercely believing in this book. It's been a joy to work on this with you. Thank you to my publisher, Jackie Dinas, who has been instrumental in championing this project since Day One. Thank you to Ann Pryor, my publicist; Stephen Smith, my production editor; Barbara Brown, for designing the most perfect cover; and the entire team at Kensington.

Special thanks to the team at Kaye Publicity, including Kaitlyn Kennedy, Katelynn Dreyer, Amanda LaConte, Ellie Imbody, and Dana Kaye.

Another joy of writing is getting to know other authors and celebrating their work. Thank you to those who have done the same for me, especially Danielle Friedman, Jessica Rotondi, Eve Rodsky, Jo Piazza, Claire Hubbard-Hall, Zibby Owens, Amaryllis Fox, David McCloskey, Alma Katsu, Pete Earley, and Frank Storey.

Thank you to my family and friends who have cheered me on through various stages of this project, especially my sister, Catherine, and brother-in-law, Mike; my stepfather, Dean; my in-laws, Ric and Sylvie; and dear friends Charise Apken, Julie Morgan, Nicole Steiner, Kristen Kish, Kate Fitzgerald, and Erick Amick. Special thanks to the OGS moms for welcoming me into this community of smart, kind, and interesting women over the past two years—your support and friendships mean the world to me.

To my dad: He's no longer with us, but if he were, he would be shouting this book from the rooftops and asking me to come speak to his local Knights of Columbus chapter. I have him to thank for my early introduction to James Bond as a little girl; I know he'd get a kick out of reading the references to Bond in this book.

And to my mom, for her endless ability to listen to me talk about my writing ideas and every other tiny thing that happens in my life on a daily basis.

Lastly, thank you to my five wonderful children, and my husband, Ryan, my first reader on everything I write and my biggest champion.

NOTES

INTRODUCTION

1   CIA, "Divine Secrets of the RYBAT Sisterhood: Four Senior Women of the Directorate of Operations Discuss Their Careers," approved for release October 30, 2013.

2   Greg Myre, "'A Woman of No Importance' Finally Gets Her Due," NPR, April 18, 2019, https://www.npr.org/2019/04/18/711356336/a-woman-of-no-importance-finally-gets-her-due.

3   Martha Peterson, interview with the author, April 5, 2023.

4   Safehouses are secure locations where operations officers meet assets. Maintaining them requires a station officer to ensure the bills are paid and to regularly visit the safehouse to make it appear as if someone actually lives there, paying close attention to utility usage so as to not raise a flag to the local intelligence service. They also keep the safehouse clean, stocked with food and beverages, and signal once they've left by doing something like leaving the blinds up or down.

5   CIA, "Divine Secrets of the RYBAT Sisterhood."

6   Debra*, interview with the author, July 6, 2023.

7   Robert Windrem, "Sisterhood of Spies: Women Now Hold the Top Positions at the CIA," NBC News, January 5, 2019, https://www.nbcnews.com/news/us-news/all-three-cia-directorates-will-now-be-headed-women-n954956.

8   United States Geospatial Intelligence Foundation (USGIF), "Dawn Meyerriecks: Central Intelligence Agency Deputy Director for Science and Technology," April 21, 2021, https://usgif.org/biography/dawn-meyerriecks/.

9   "Director's Diversity in Leadership Study," 2019, https://www.cia.gov/static/6c3dcb22cd19b11dbd8352082286f225/DLS_Year_4_Report.pdf.

10 Deb Riechmann, "CIA's New Recruitment Website Aims to Diversify Spy Agency," AP News, January 4, 2021, https://apnews.com/article/technology-business-race-and-ethnicity-intelligence-agencies-demographics-e22ea4d22d4564608d7972be95e570b9.

11 "Director's Diversity in Leadership Study."

CHAPTER 1

1   Brett Durbin, "Addressing 'This Woeful Imbalance': Efforts to Improve Women's Representation at CIA, 1947–2013," Government: Faculty Publications, Smith College, October 30, 2013.

2   "Executive Orders," Richard Nixon Presidential Library and Museum, accessed October 1, 2023, https://www.nixonlibrary.gov/president/executive-orders.

3   Durbin, "Addressing 'This Woeful Imbalance.'"

4   Debra*, interview with the author, July 6, 2023.

5   Field tradecraft certification (FTC), also referred to as "operational certification" ("ops-certified"), is the name of the intense, months-long training course operations officers are required to complete at the CIA's covert training facility, the Farm.

6   Ann Donohue, interview with the author, June 16, 2023.

7   Terry Kees, interview with the author, July 14, 2023.

8   CIA, "Divine Secrets of the RYBAT Sisterhood: Four Senior Women of the Directorate of Operations Discuss Their Careers," approved for release October 30, 2013.

9   Susan Amato, interview with the author, May 26, 2023.

10 *Frontline*, "Hillary's Class," produced by Rachel Dretzin and Jane West, aired November 15, 1994, on PBS, https://www.pbs.org/wgbh/frontline/documentary/hillarys-class/.

11 Lucy Kirk, interview.

12 Ibid.

13 *Frontline*, "Hillary's Class."

14 Lucy Kirk, interview.

15 Ibid.

16 Ibid.

17 Ibid.

18 Ibid.

19 Ibid.

20 Ibid.

21 Sue McCloud, interview with the author, July 2, 2023.

22 Judy Sholes, interview with the author, July 13, 2023.

23 Sue McCloud, interview.

24 CIA, "Divine Secrets of the RYBAT Sisterhood."

25 Sue McCloud, interview.

26 Steven Brookner, interview with the author, May 18, 2023.

27 Art Katcher, interview with the author, May 19, 2023.

28 George Amato, interview with the author, May 23, 2023.

29 Richard Sandomir, "Janine Brookner, Punished C.I.A. Officer Who Got Revenge, Dies at 80," *New York Times*, May 26, 2021, https://www.nytimes.com/2021/05/26/us/janine-brookner-dead.html.

30 Colin Thompson, interview with the author, May 18, 2023.

31 Abigail Jones, "She Was a CIA Spy. Now She's a Lawyer Battling Her Old Agency. This Is Her Story," *Washington Post*, June 5, 2018, https://www.washingtonpost.com/lifestyle/magazine/she-was-a-cia-spy-now-shes-a-lawyer-battling-her-old-agency-this-is-her-story/2018/06/01/5784f45e-5abe-11e8-858f-12becb4d6067_story.html.

32 Colin Thompson, interview.

33 Sandomir, "Janine Brookner."

34 Jones, "She Was a CIA Spy."

35 Matt Schudel, "Janine Brookner, Ousted CIA Officer Who Challenged Agency in Court, Dies at 80," *Washington Post*, May 14, 2021, https://www.washingtonpost.com/local/obituaries/janine-brookner-dead/2021/05/14/98b87320-b406-11eb-9059-d8176b9e3798_story.html.

36   Colin Thompson, interview.

37   Sandomir, "Janine Brookner."

38   Jones, "She Was a CIA Spy."

39   Schudel, "Janine Brookner."

40   Martha Peterson, interview with the author, April 5, 2023.

41   Amy Tozzi, interview with the author, July 5, 2023.

42   Debra*, interview with the author, July 6, 2023.

43   Terry Kees, interview.

44   Martha Peterson, interview with the author, April 5, 2023.

CHAPTER 2

1   "WOMEN OF THE YEAR: Great Changes, New Chances, Tough Choices," *Time*, January 6, 1976, https://time.com/archive/6595056/women-of-the-year-great-changes-new-chances-tough-choices/.

2   Mark Cerulli, "Part I of Mark Cerulli's Interview with Gloria Hendry: The Movies," March 24, 2024, https://jamesbond007.se/eng/intervjuer/gloria_hendry_interview_the_movies.

3   Carmen Medina, interview with the author, June 16, 2023.

4   Ibid.

5   The US Merit Systems Protection Board, "A Question of Equity: Women and the Glass Ceiling in the Federal Government," a report to the President and the Congress of the United States, October 1992, https://www.mspb.gov/studies/studies/A_Question_of_Equity_Women_and_the_Glass_Ceiling_in_the_Federal_Government_280689.pdf.

6   Margery, interview with the author, June 24, 2023.

7   Ibid.

8   Martha D. Peterson, *The Widow Spy* (Red Canary Press, 2012).

9   Ibid.

10   Jessica Pearce Rotondi, "Why Laos Has Been Bombed More Than Any Other Country," History Channel, August 11, 2023, https://www.history.com/news/laos-most-bombed-country-vietnam-war.

11 Peterson, *Widow Spy*.

12 Martha Peterson, interview with the author, April 5, 2023.

13 Rotondi, "Why Laos Has Been Bombed."

14 "Vietnam War U.S. Military Fatal Casualty Statistics," National Archives, accessed April 5, 2023, https://www.archives.gov /research/military/vietnam-war/casualty-statistics#water.

15 Peterson, *Widow Spy*.

16 Martha Peterson, interview.

17 Peterson, *Widow Spy*.

18 Martha Peterson, interview.

19 Lucy Kirk, *We Already Have a Woman We Like: My Life in the CIA*, Decktora Press, 2024.

20 Lucy Kirk, interview with the author, May 22, 2023.

21 Amy Tozzi, interview with the author, July 5, 2023.

22 Katherine Layton, interview with the author, July 6, 2023.

23 Debra*, interview with the author, July 6, 2023.

24 Making it to the Senior Intelligence Service (SIS)—the level beyond a GS-15—is an incredible accomplishment for any CIA officer, but it's particularly notable as a woman at the CIA and considerably rarer for female officers working in operations.

25 Sharon Bassom, interview with the author, July 6, 2023.

26 Colin Thompson, interview with the author, May 18, 2023.

27 Richard Sandomir, "Janine Brookner, Punished C.I.A. Officer Who Got Revenge, Dies at 80," *New York Times*, May 26, 2021, https://www.nytimes.com/2021/05/26/us/janine-brookner-dead .html.

28 Abigail Jones, "She Was a CIA Spy. Now She's a Lawyer Battling Her Old Agency. This Is Her Story," *Washington Post*, June 5, 2018, https://www.washingtonpost.com/lifestyle/magazine/she-was -a-cia-spy-now-shes-a-lawyer-battling-her-old-agency-this-is -her-story/2018/06/01/5784f45e-5abe-11e8-858f-12becb4d6067 _story.html.

29 Matt Schudel, "Janine Brookner, Ousted CIA Officer Who Challenged Agency in Court, Dies at 80," *Washington Post*, May 14, 2021, https://www.washingtonpost.com/local/obituaries/janine -brookner-dead/2021/05/14/98b87320-b406-11eb-9059 -d8176b9e3798_story.html.

30   Colin Thompson, interview.

31   Ann Donohue, interview with the author, June 16, 2023.

32   Colin Thompson, interview.

33   George Amato, interview with the author, May 23, 2023.

34   Susan Amato, interview with the author, May 26, 2023.

35   Colin Thompson, interview.

36   Schudel, "Janine Brookner."

37   Colin Thompson, interview with the author, May 18, 2023.

38   Ibid.

39   Ibid.

40   David Binder, "Turner Begins Personnel Cuts in the C.I.A.'s Clandestine Services," *New York Times*, November 13, 1977, https://www.cia.gov/readingroom/docs/CIA-RDP99-00498R0001001 20061-4.pdf.

41   Susan Amato, interview with the author, May 16, 2023.

CHAPTER 3

1   Lesley Kennedy, "Five Pop Culture Trends That Helped Shape the 1980s," History, updated October 2, 2023, https://www.history.com/news/1980s-pop-culture-trends.

2   Carmen Medina, interview with the author, June 16, 2023.

3   Ibid.

4   Carol F., interview with the author, June 30, 2023.

5   Lucy Kirk, interview with the author, May 22, 2023.

6   Richard Sandomir, "Janine Brookner, Punished C.I.A. Officer Who Got Revenge, Dies at 80," *New York Times*, May 26, 2021, https://www.nytimes.com/2021/05/26/us/janine-brookner-dead.html.

7   Colin Thompson, interview with the author, May 18, 2023.

8   Sandomir, "Janine Brookner."

9   Abigail Jones, "She Was a CIA Spy. Now She's a Lawyer Battling Her Old Agency. This Is Her Story," *Washington Post*, June 5, 2018, https://www.washingtonpost.com/lifestyle/magazine/she-was-a

-cia-spy-now-shes-a-lawyer-battling-her-old-agency-this-is-her
-story/2018/06/01/5784f45e-5abe-11e8-858f-12becb4d6067
_story.html.

10 Matt Schudel, "Janine Brookner, Ousted CIA Officer Who Challenged Agency in Court, Dies at 80," *Washington Post*, May 14,
2021, https://www.washingtonpost.com/local/obituaries/janine
-brookner-dead/2021/05/14/98b87320-b406-11eb-9059-
d8176b9e3798_story.html.

11 Angela S., interview with the author, May 23, 2023.

12 Colin Thompson, interview.

13 Sandomir, "Janine Brookner."

14 Jones, "She Was a CIA Spy."

15 Schudel, "Janine Brookner."

16 Susan Kiely, interview with the author, May 23, 2023.

17 Retired female case officer, interview with the author, June 2,
2023.

18 Angela S. interview.

19 Colin Thompson, interview.

20 Ibid.

21 Ibid.

22 Sandomir, "Janine Brookner."

23 Carmen Medina, interview with the author, June 16, 2023.

24 Angela S., interview.

25 Jones, "She Was a CIA Spy."

26 Colin Thompson, interview.

27 Sandomir, "Janine Brookner."

28 David Wise, "Spy vs. Spies," *Los Angeles Times*, July 21, 1996,
https://www.latimes.com/archives/la-xpm-1996-07-21-tm
-26281-story.html.

29 Jones, "She Was a CIA Spy."

30 Colin Thompson, interview.

31 Sandomir, "Janine Brookner."

32 Wise, "Spy vs. Spies."

33 Ibid.

34　Colin Thompson, interview.

35　Jones, "She Was a CIA Spy."

36　Colin Thompson, interview.

37　Sandomir, "Janine Brookner."

38　Wise, "Spy vs. Spies."

39　Colin Thompson, interview.

40　Margery, interview with the author, June 24, 2023.

41　Schudel, "Janine Brookner."

42　CIA, "Divine Secrets of the RYBAT Sisterhood: Four Senior Women of the Directorate of Operations Discuss Their Careers," approved for release October 30, 2013.

43　Ibid.

44　Ibid.

45　Mary Beth Long, interview with the author, June 2, 2023.

46　Ibid.

47　The "Bubble" refers to the CIA's headquarters auditorium.

48　CIA, "Divine Secrets of the RYBAT Sisterhood."

49　Carmen Medina, interview.

50　Debra*, interview with the author, July 6, 2023.

CHAPTER 4

1　Allison Yarrow, "How the '90s Tricked Women into Thinking They'd Gained Gender Equality," *Time*, June 13, 2018, https://time.com/5310256/90s-gender-equality-progress/.

2　Ibid.

3　Amanda Hess, "'Ditsy, Predatory White House Intern,'" *Slate*, May 7, 2014, https://slate.com/human-interest/2014/05/monica-lewinsky-returns-how-maureen-dowd-caricatured-bill-clintons-mistress-as-a-crazy-bimbo.html.

4　Jessica Bennett, "The Shaming of Monica: Why We Owe Her an Apology," *Time*, May 9, 2014, https://time.com/92989/monica-lewinsky-slut-shaming-feminists-media-apology/.

5　Tatiana Siegel, "Why 'Bond' Mogul Barbara Broccoli Has Earned a License to Chill," *Hollywood Reporter*, December 7, 2021,

https://www.hollywoodreporter.com/movies/movie-features
/barbara-broccoli-profile-james-bond-1235058174/.

6   Lucy Kirk, interview with the author, May 22, 2023.

7   Ibid.

8   Abigail Jones, "She Was a CIA Spy. Now She's a Lawyer Battling
    Her Old Agency. This Is Her Story," *Washington Post*, June 5, 2018,
    https://www.washingtonpost.com/lifestyle/magazine/she-was-a
    -cia-spy-now-shes-a-lawyer-battling-her-old-agency-this-is-her
    -story/2018/06/01/5784f45e-5abe-11e8-858f-12becb4d6067
    _story.html.

9   Wise, "Spy vs. Spies."

10 Sandomir, "Janine Brookner."

11 David Wise, "Spy vs. Spies," *Los Angeles Times*. July 21, 1996.
    https://www.latimes.com/archives/la-xpm-1996-07-21-tm
    -26281-story.html.

12 Richard Sandomir, "Janine Brookner, Punished CIA Officer
    Who Got Revenge, Dies at 80," *New York Times*, May 26, 2021,
    https://www.nytimes.com/2021/05/26/us/janine-brookner
    -dead.html.

13 Jones, "She Was a CIA Spy."

14 Wise, "Spy vs. Spies."

15 Robert Pear, "C.I.A. Settles Suit on Sex Bias," *New York Times*,
    March 30, 1995, https://www.nytimes.com/1995/03/30/us/cia
    -settles-suit-on-sex-bias.html.

16 Margery, interview with the author, June 24, 2023.

17 Carmen Medina, interview with the author, June 16, 2023.

18 Former case officer, interview with the author.

19 Margery, interview.

20 Megan S., interview with the author, May 10, 2023.

21 Ibid.

22 Lucy Kirk, interview.

23 Lebanon. CIA World Factbook. Accessed June 3, 2022. https://
    www.cia.gov/the-world-factbook/countries/lebanon/.

24 "Joint CIA-FBI Press Release on Arrest of Harold James Nichol-
    son," November 18, 1996, https://irp.fas.org/cia/news/pr111896
    .html

CHAPTER 5

1   Erin El Issa, "Women and Credit Through the Decades: The 2000s," *Nerd Wallet*, updated July 12, 2023, https://www.nerdwallet .com/article/credit-cards/women-credit-decades-00s.

2   Britney Spears, interview by Diane Sawyer, *Primetime*, ABC, November 13, 2003.

3   Britney Spears, interview by Matt Lauer, *Dateline*, NBC, June 15, 2006.

4   Spears, interview with Sawyer.

5   Gina Bennett, interview with the author, May 2, 2023.

6   Ibid.

7   Megan S., interview with the author, May 10, 2023.

8   Priscila, interview with the author, June 10, 2023.

9   Mary S., interview with the author, March 1, 2023.

10   Kathleen, interview with the author, March 8, 2023.

11   Gina Bennett, interview.

CHAPTER 6

1   "Spectre Interview—Lea Seydoux (2015)—James Bond Movie HD," posted November 4, 2015, by Rotten Tomatoes Coming Soon, https://www.youtube.com/watch?v=gP0TI4i84Hg.

2   CIA, "Director's Advisory Group on Women in Leadership, Unclassified Report," March 2013, https://www.cia.gov/static /825c79d82205d8b8e0045a8dd87fc614/CIA_Women_In _Leadership_March2013.pdf.

3   Interviews with the author, CIA headquarters, June 22, 2023.

4   "Director's Advisory Group."

5   As part of this reorganization, the Directorate of Intelligence, or DI, was also renamed as the Directorate of Analysis, or DA.

6   Mary S., interview with the author, March 1, 2023.

7   "Director's Advisory Group."

8   Ibid.

9   Unnamed CIA officer, interview with the author, June 2023.

10 Author interviews at CIA headquarters. June 22, 2023.

11 Laura Thomas, interview with the author, June 19, 2023.

12 Laura Thomas, "Espionage Is a Man's World: Sex, Lies, and the CIA," *The Action Line* (blog), August 8, 2023, https://www.laurae thomas.com/p/espionage-is-a-mans-world.

13 Laura Thomas, interview.

14 "Tracey Ballard: Breaking Through Cultural Barriers to Serve Her Country," INTEL.gov., accessed May 19, 2023, https://www.intelligence.gov/people/current-barrier-breakers/427-tracey-ballard.

15 Elyse, interview with the author, December 17, 2023.

16 Senior DO officer, interview with the author, February 2, 2024.

17 Rebecca Shabad, "Senate Confirms Gina Haspel as CIA Director," NBC News, May 17, 2018, https://www.nbcnews.com/politics/congress/senate-confirms-gina-haspel-cia-director-n875141.

18 Robert Windrem, "Beth Kimber Becomes First Woman to Run the CIA's Clandestine Operations," NBC News, December 7, 2018, https://www.nbcnews.com/politics/national-security/spy-mistress-beth-kimber-becomes-first-woman-run-cia-s-n945456.

19 Olivia Gazis, "CIA Director Gina Haspel Announces New Leadership Picks," CBS News, August 22, 2018, https://www.cbsnews.com/news/cia-director-gina-haspel-announces-new-leadership-picks/.

20 Ibid.

CHAPTER 7

1   Jessica Bennett, "Monica Lewinsky Is (Reluctantly) Revisiting 'That Woman,'" *New York Times*, September 1, 2021, https://www.nytimes.com/2021/09/01/arts/television/monica-lewinsky-impeachment-american-crime-story.html.

2   Julia Jacobs, "Britney Spears, From the Conservatorship's Demise to 'The Woman in Me,'" *New York Times*, October 20, 2023, https://www.nytimes.com/2023/10/20/arts/music/britney-spears-timeline-conservatorship-memoir.html.

3   Julia Jacobs, "Britney Spears's Memoir Sells 1.1 Million Copies in the U.S. First Week," *New York Times*, November 1, 2023, https://www.nytimes.com/2023/11/01/arts/music/britney-spears-memoir-woman-in-me-sales.html#:~:text=Britney%20Spears's%20much%2Danticipated%20memoir,Gallery%20Books%2C%20announced%20on%20Wednesday.

4   Johnny Diaz, "Ex-C.I.A. Officer Gets 30 Years for Drugging and Sexually Assaulting Women," *New York Times*, September 19, 2024, https://www.nytimes.com/2024/09/19/us/brian-jeffrey-raymond-cia-sexual-assault.html.

5   Mary S., interview with the author, March 17, 2022.

6   Elyse, interview with the author, January 5, 2024.

7   Elyse, interview with the author, December 17, 2023.

8   Daniel Lippman, "Under Fire, CIA Moves to Overhaul Its Handling of Sexual Assault," *Politico*. May 11, 2023, https://www.politico.com/news/2023/05/11/cia-moves-to-overhaul-handling-of-sexual-assault-00096498.

9   Elyse, interview with the author, December 17, 2023.

EPILOGUE

1   Laurel Wamsley, "Michelle Obama's Take On 'Lean In'? 'That &#%! Doesn't Work,'" NPR. December 3, 2018, https://www.npr.org/2018/12/03/672898216/michelle-obamas-take-on-lean-in-that-doesn-t-work

2   Sue Gordon, interview with the author, December 22, 2023.

3   Ibid.

4   Ibid.

5   "Director's Diversity in Leadership Study: Overcoming Barriers to Advancement," https://www.cia.gov/static/d8681a6dc204460 42a8c3020459ca1d4/Directors-Diversity-in-Leadership-Study-Overcoming-Barriers-to-Advancement.pdf.

6   The CIA's Office of Public Affairs would not confirm this and was unable, or unwilling, to provide a breakdown by directorate of women of color in the SIS.

7   "Challenging the Status Quo: Elizabeth Sudmeier's Historic Legacy," CIA. June 26, 2015, https://www.cia.gov/stories/story /elizabeth-sudmeier/#despite-successes-hurdles-remain.